Asymmetric Alliances and Information Systems

Advances in Information Systems Set

coordinated by
Camille Rosenthal-Sabroux

Volume 7

Asymmetric Alliances and Information Systems

Issues and Prospects

Karim Saïd
Fadia Bahri Korbi

WILEY

First published 2017 in Great Britain and the United States by ISTE Ltd and John Wiley & Sons, Inc.

ISTE Ltd
27-37 St George's Road
London SW19 4EU
UK

www.iste.co.uk

John Wiley & Sons, Inc.
111 River Street
Hoboken, NJ 07030
USA

www.wiley.com

Library of Congress Control Number: 2017935629

British Library Cataloguing-in-Publication Data
A CIP record for this book is available from the British Library
ISBN 978-1-78630-097-3

Contents

Introduction

The number of international strategic alliances has grown considerably in recent years due to the increase in interdependency between economies resulting from the globalization of goods and services and financial markets. Subsequently, companies have had to reinforce their international strategic deployment capabilities, which have been made possible by the development of new generations of information and communications technologies. Academia has responded to this boom in strategic alliances with an abundance of research dedicated to this new theme, particularly in fields such as management sciences and industrial economics. And yet there are but few of these studies that focus on the management of asymmetric alliances, in particular between multinational corporations and companies from emerging economies[1]. A strategic alliance can be defined as a link between two or more individual companies with different sizes, resources and capacities originating from geographic areas characterized by uneven levels of macroeconomic development [MOU 05]. An asymmetric alliance is based on a number asymmetry criteria relying on geographic location, differences in size,

---

1 United Nations, Department of Economic and Social Affairs, World Urbanization Prospects, the 2011 Revision, File 5 Total Population: http://esa.un.org/unup/CD-ROM/ Urban-Rural-Population.htm.

capital and negotiating power or even experience in domestic or international collaborations and the ability to learn from one's partners.

Coordinating the activities of a strategic alliance is increasingly complex when it ties asymmetric partners separated by strategic decisions and managerial systems set in specific social and cultural contexts. These differences can be amplified by the geographic distance that separates the partners, increasing the need for joint activity to be appropriately coordinated.

In this context, the use of an integrated information system can help unify shared information between collaborators and allow them to develop a common framework, reducing problems stemming from informational asymmetry and incompatibility within the alliance. In their ability to reduce the restrictions related to spatial locations, information systems help reduce the costs of acquisition and transportation as well as the costs of coordinating activities spanning different locations. They, therefore, encourage massive exchanges of data as well as increases in productivity and reactivity in decision making.

As we look closer at the integration of information systems within asymmetric strategic alliances, we will study the role of these technologies as tools for workflow management, communication and sharing and collaboration between geographically distant stakeholders working toward common goals.

This book is divided into two parts. Part 1 presents the specificities of asymmetric strategic alliances and will define the intellectual context of the information system and its formal and informal role in guiding strategic alliances. Part 2 is dedicated to case studies and will describe the role of information systems in managing asymmetric alliances. The organizational structure of the alliance, the ends and resources put forward by each party, their position in the value chain of the alliance and the selected mode of governance is presented for each case. We will then analyze the role of the information system in the formal and informal governance of said alliance. The detailed analyses of these cases will allow us to make managerial recommendations relating to the importance of information systems in communications within and between businesses, enlightened governance and decision making as well as the management of common information.

Specificities of IS within Asymmetric Alliances

Introduction to Part 1

After the diffusion of integrative technologies within businesses, the question of information system integration moved to the field of relations across organizations, where it generates more and more interest among researchers in Information Systems (IS) management. The study of interorganizational relations has recently become far more interesting due to the appearance of strategic alliances and partnerships, as opposed to the traditional dichotomization of straight market and hierarchy in conjunction with the increasing use of IS. These technologies are capable of managing the relations between partners and supporting their formal and informal governance methods because of a combination of material and non-physical resources.

However, coordinating the activities of a strategic alliance is all the more complex when it links partners that are asymmetric with regard to the differences or even incompatibilities between their strategic decisions and managerial systems, often set in specific social and cultural structures. These differences can be amplified by the geographic distance between partners, highlighting the need to coordinate joint activities.

In this context, an integrated information system can unify the information shared between partners and help develop a common framework that will work toward problems arising from information asymmetry and incompatibility within the alliance. Through their ability to alleviate restrictions linked to spatial location, information systems can help reduce the costs of acquisition and transportation of information, thus enhancing efficiency and productivity as well as decision-making time. Furthermore, these technologies allow the development of interpersonal relations between the members of two partnering companies and the establishment of a dynamic of knowledge transfer.

Strategic Alliances versus Asymmetric Alliances

1.1. Strategic alliances

A cooperation agreement between organizations relies on a range of partnership relations between corporations that seek to realize a joint production of information, products or commercial services. These agreements include different forms of contractual cooperation such as licensing contracts, R&D agreements and functional collaborations that aim to reinforce the value chain of both parties which can range from common participations to total integration (see Figure 1.1). This can be a number of autonomous entities participating in a network, applying one of many possible configurations: corporate collaboration – cooperation between two or more partners from different countries where each corporation remains autonomous within the areas that are not included within the collaboration perimeters including the common realization of activities and specific tasks.

Garrette and Dussauge [GAR 95] present an analysis grid of different forms of collaborations for strategic alliances, thus distinguishing agreements between competing corporations from agreements between non-competing corporations. A distinction can thus be made between market relations, mergers and acquisitions, and collaborations (see Table 1.1). The following analysis grid presents the differences in definitions of collaboration and the collaboration models between corporations. We will note that one of the most ubiquitous collaboration models remains is that of strategic alliance.

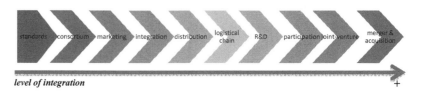

level of integration   +

Figure 1.1. *Configurations of alliances (Alliance Science, 2004)*

Stakeholders Relation	Non-competing corporations			Competing corporations
Market relations	Exports and imports	Transactions		Competition
Mergers and acquisitions	Local acquisitions	Vertical integration	Diversification	Sector concentration
Collaboration	Multinationalization *joint venture*	Vertical partnerships	Intersectoral agreement	Strategic alliances between competitors

Table 1.1. *Analysis grid of the forms of relations and interorganization cooperation (source [GAR 95, p. 97])*

1.1.1. *Definition*

The notion of strategic alliance refers to a link between two or more individual corporations, deciding on the governance and structure of a common project while both maintaining their independence. They are therefore engaged in a partnership whereby they will share the benefits and the costs of the collaboration. Khanna *et al.* [KHA 98, p. 195] highlight other dimensions associated with the definition of alliance, citing the mutual transfer of information between strategic partners and the development of organizational knowledge. Resorting to strategic alliances is here justified by the act of: "mutually transferring information from one partner to another, allowing them to combine and grow their competences and key-knowledge to exploit them within common operations". However, Gulati [GUL 98] highlights goals other than the transfer of knowledge and learning, such as the desire to exchange, share or develop common products, technologies or services.

Jolly [JOL 01, p. 3], on the other hand, defines alliances as:

> "A link established by at least two sovereign companies that do not belong to the same group, agreeing to pursue a common goal within a defined space by pooling or exchanging resources in order to obtain mutually beneficial results, while remaining independent outside of the alliance".

This notion of independence implies, for the partners, that they maintain their strategic autonomy outside of the areas covered by the mutual agreements. For their part, Contractor and Lorange [CON 88] put forward the importance of sharing financial and technological resources as well as the management and control model of the joint activity. Pooling complementary capital and manpower as well as production capabilities and information must therefore allow the creation of value [BUC 88].

Using these definitions as a basis, we can establish a theoretical framework that encompasses the different dimensions that characterize a strategic alliance, i.e.:

– a strategic alliance encourages networking between non-competing companies, competing companies or potentially competing companies;

– the decision to enter a strategic alliance must involve a formal, well-defined and appropriately structured contract;

– when active, this contract will not remove the autonomy of either of the companies or their independence;

– a strategic alliance involves pooling resources and capabilities as well as sharing the results by the contracting parties.

1.1.2. *Organizational forms*

Partnerships, functional collaborations, joint ventures and cooperation agreements are generic terms that refer to various organizational forms that companies can take on in order to mobilize the resources necessary to their competitiveness. These organizational forms can fall into one of two categories depending on whether the nature of the commitment is equity based or simply contractual.

1.1.2.1. *Equity alliances*

Joint ventures and equity investments (joint/unilateral) are representative of this type of alliance. Joint ventures, in particular, refer to the investment of capital into a new entity and the pooling of resources among a number of partners. This will take the form of a new administrative structure that operates on the basis of a new hierarchy. The objectives for a joint venture are most often expressed in a long-term context in the areas of R&D, production and product commercialization. Kogut [KOG 88], Pisano [PIS 89, PIS 91] and even Oxley [OXL 97] mention that joint ventures allow control over the behaviors of the partners in order to align their objectives, particularly in the context of an uncertain environment favorable to opportunistic moves and behaviors.

Members of a joint venture agree beforehand to commit their resources in order to determine ownership over the common subsidiary. This avoids any of the partners going back on their commitment. Furthermore, the partners wield their operational power via a formal administrative unit (the executive board of the joint venture), which allows them to efficiently exercise control over the joint activity and reduce transaction costs among partners.

Das and Teng [DAS 98] underline the fact that joint ventures allow control over decisions, resources, assets and partners through specific organizational routines and an elevated hierarchical control. This type of alliance ensures that the partners' interests are aligned and reduces the inherent costs that occur from incomplete contracts and opportunistic behaviors.

The works of Contractor and Lorange [CON 88, p. 6] emphasize the high level of co-dependency between partners during a joint venture who mobilize part of their personnel in a collaborative framework and rely on common resources, technologies and processes: "The joint venture is a cooperative arrangement characterized by a high level of organizational interdependency". Therefore, the partners are in constant interaction at all hierarchical levels in order to optimize the exchange of knowledge and expertise and to simultaneously direct added-value operations [GUL 98]. This is manifested by an integration of abilities and resources by both contracting parties allowing them to synergize in terms of commercialization capabilities, production capacities or even research and development.

Park and Russo [PAR 96] differentiate "integrated" forms from "sequential" forms of alliance depending on the nature of the interdependency of the partners. Therefore, the "integrated" joint venture is characterized by a joint interdependency between partners since they dedicate part of their personnel and resources to an integrated and separate organization, granting them an operational role. On the other hand, "sequential" joint ventures are characterized by a "sequential" interdependency in the sense that operations are directly taken on by members of the alliance. Each partner performs the distinct actions that are tied to the resources they commit before transferring activity to a partner who continues the work using on their own resources. With common venture not having an operational role, it is confined to a role of judicial and administrative coordination. As for Hennart [HEN 88], he distinguishes between scale joint ventures and link joint ventures. This is based on the transaction cost theory [WIL 85]. While the former model of alliance aims to realize similar economies of scale by pooling similar resources, the latter is preferred by companies with complementary resources with the objective of developing activity synergies.

Recourse to equity alliances is favorable when partners are looking to exchange or acquire new skills. Khanna *et al.* [KHA 98] point out that successful knowledge transfer and learning requires a solid governance of the alliance allowing the partners to effectively perform R&D activities. In the same vein, Mowery *et al.* [MOW 96] emphasize that tacit knowledge requires a large amount of interactions, personal relations and proximity between partners. Competence transfer activities are assisted by the presence of executives dedicated to joint ventures as well as face-to-face meetings and improved personal relations between partners. Asymmetric strategic alliances that connect partners from cultures from different geographical contexts need to be governed by equity agreements that encourage learning and the acquisition of knowledge, unlike contractual agreements [LI 09].

Furthermore, it should be noted in this context that joint ventures are most often associated with high investment costs relating to equipment, personnel or the creation of a new managerial structure designed to direct the joint activities. The particularly irrecoverable nature of these investments as well as the elevated exit costs of these types of alliances reduces the ability for partners to adapt to unpredicted events or develop an innovation dynamic likely to encourage the development of new products and/or processes.

1.1.2.2. Contractual alliances

Contractual alliances refer to agreements established between partners to cooperate while maintaining their autonomy and without creating a new entity. Contractual alliances are preferred by companies operating within a context of high uncertainty and adapted to the knowledge transfer and expertise associated with activities in the technological sector [HAG 02]. Companies therefore favor contractual agreements such as licenses in intensive R1D sectors, where technological innovations are both radical and constantly changing. The simplicity of management and the flexibility offered by contractual alliances help the negotiations and collaboration between different parties [HAG 96].

Contractual alliances allow the protection of new knowledge while transferring anything essential to the alliance. Using a study of 271 cases of equitable "joint venture" alliances and non-equitable "unilateral and bi-lateral contract" alliances, entered into by American, European and Japanese companies, Colombo [COL 03] shows that the probability of resorting to a joint venture decreases with the existence of similar knowledge and technological capabilities among partners. The latter will prioritize equity-based forms whenever the alliance involves a unilateral transfer of resources and competences in favor of one of the parties.

Characterized by a high level of organizational independence among members [GUL 98], contractual collaborations imply few exchanges of information and knowledge, as well as a low-level operational interaction among the stakeholders. The studies performed by Das and Teng [DAS 08] as well as by Chen and Chen [CHE 03] demonstrate that contractual alliances are preferred by small-scale entities looking to perform economies of scale on partially outsourced activities that do not require the integration of resources or key competencies.

1.1.3. *Objectives set by the partners*

Recourse to a strategic alliance is most often driven by the desire to convert a potential market competitor into a partner; to receive material, financial or human assistance; or to develop technical, technological or financial synergies. A number of authors [HAR 85, TEE 86, HEN 88, KOG 88, WIL 91] have studied the motivations that explain the formation of a strategic alliance, which we will classify according to their expected results in the following sections.

1.1.3.1. *Reducing transaction costs*

Any economic transaction generates costs prior to its realization, tying in with the costs linked to information, to "market deficiencies", to preventing opportunism from other agents, etc. Hence, certain transactions taking place on the market can generate high transaction costs. This can lead to financial agents seeking alternative institutional arrangements which enable them to minimize these costs. The transaction costs approach, developed by economics pioneer Coase [COA 37], accentuates the importance of hierarchies as an alternative mode of support for transactions. At the other end of the market, Williamson [WIL 91] follows Coase in distinguishing "hierarchy", which generally corresponds to the company. Between the market and the company, there are a number of "hybrid" forms that can be identified (subcontracting, franchising, network, etc.). According to Ménard [MÉN 97], these "hybrid forms" or "networks" refer to:

"A diverse number of arrangements such as franchises, long-term inter-business contracts, business networks, which are given coherence by identifying their common characteristics such as the partial transfer of power to allocate resources without transferring the property rights" [MÉN 97, p. 742].

In hybrid form, strategic alliances sit alongside the principles established by the founders of the transaction costs approach.

Companies opt for the solution of an alliance in order to reduce the level of uncertainty that comes with certain market transactions, maximize the usage of specific assets and face opportunistic behaviors of economic agents. A strategic alliance appears as the more appropriate option in order to realize economies of scale while simultaneously avoiding the use of market systems that would generate high costs tied to pricing research, negotiation and drafting (*ex ante* transaction costs) or even contract compliance (*ex post* transaction costs).

The strategic alliance option is justified, not only by how it reduces transaction costs, but also in the specificity of assets required. If assets are very specific then increases in transactions inevitably become very costly. It therefore makes sense to group them within a single organization in order to reduce transaction costs. However, opportunism and uncertainty rise as soon as the number of actors is low and when there are few transactions between partners. Hence, why corporations opt for strategic alliances to reduce transaction costs tied with market uncertainty.

1.1.3.2. *Resource acquisition and dependence*

The resource-based view has often been used to explain the decision of businesses to form a strategic alliance [BAR 91, PRA 90]. This approach states that the formation of an alliance depends on the potential for value generation of the resources placed in common by two allied corporations. The alliance is presented as the strategic option, enabling the acquisition of new competitive advantages and value creation [POR 86]. These alliances are established by companies in an aim to access new resources that they do not possess or could not obtain individually, such as access to new international markets, strategic resources that would be hard to duplicate or transfer and the development of new abilities and competencies. It is in this vein that alliances provide opportunities for value creation.

According to the resource-based view, the key to competitive advantage is to be found within the company. The latter is therefore encouraged to adopt a dynamic which will allow it to reinforce its catalog of resources and capabilities and acquire those it needs for future development. These resources are considered strategic whereupon they contribute to the development of abilities and key competencies of the company [TEE 97]. Resources can be categorized as either tangible resources (for instance, any financial, human or physical resources) or intangible (expertise, reputation, technologies, managerial experience, for example). Disparity remains the essential factor for distinguishing between companies. This element constitutes the basis of the resource-based view.

Beyond the aforementioned resource sharing, companies can form allegiances in order to share commercial resources based on reputation, notoriety and customer relations. The created value therefore results from an improved global performance, growth, conquering new market shares, increasing area of activity, increased margins in terms of volume and/or value, etc.

The theory of resource dependence analyzes the development of intercompany relations through two key variables: dependence and uncertainty [PFE 78]. The level of dependence of one company toward another depends on the importance, the specificity and the availability of the resources held (for example capital, expertise, personnel, etc.). The inability for one company to manage its resource flows will further increase its perceived environmental uncertainty.

Therefore, the members of an alliance seek to manage uncertainty issues by establishing formal or semiformal relations with other companies. These relations allow them to decrease their vulnerability vis-à-vis their environment and properly manage their dependence toward it. A company's perceived vulnerability to its environment is a function of its needs in terms of human, financial, technical and informational resources; in other words, resources controlled by its environment. The level of dependence of a company on its environment reinforces the power of the latter, which will then dictate its demands, in particular competitive rates, products and services fulfilling its needs, structures and specific organizational processes.

In this approach, strategic alliances are seen as a maneuver that will allow a company to gain power by minimizing its dependence on its environment. According to Pfeffer and Salancik [PFE 78], the level of dependence determines the amount of power of each party in a cross-organizational relationship. A company holds a large amount of power if the operation of the alliance depends entirely on its input in terms of tangible and intangible resources. The nature of the inputs of the partners therefore dictates their negotiating power within the alliance [HAR 85]. The control over key resources by one company therefore represents a source of deciding power within the partnership.

1.1.3.3. Learning

The organizational learning theory has been used by a number of researchers in the past two decades to analyze the formation of strategic alliances [KOG 88, DOZ 98, KHA 98, SIM 04]. Doz et al. [DOZ 89] see strategic alliances as a way to appropriate competences and expertise from partner companies through learning processes. It states that strategic alliances enable the fast acquisition of new knowledge at reduced costs, thus contributing to the strategic consolidation of a company.

EXAMPLE.– Indian companies have formed alliances with American corporations in order to acquire new abilities and expertise in the areas of IT and information and communications technology (ICT). Through these partnerships, India's industry became the first to promote a "global outsourcing of services model". Indian exports of IT services and ICT-related services have grown considerably because of the superiority in terms of quality and price offered by Indian companies in comparison to their competitors. Over time, Indian industries have become capable of taking on entire IT projects for overseas clients.

A company's absorptive capacity [COH 90] rests on its ability to determine, assess, assimilate and apply new knowledge according to its prior knowledge and investments on which it can rely. Past experience, as well as being at the center of information exchanges, will also tangibly improve a company's absorptive capacity. This dynamic ability [TEE 97] is essential to developing new knowledge and engaging a dynamic of organizational learning. Thus, a company's "retention capacity" determines the success of its learning process [SZU 96]. This refers to a receiver's ability to institutionalize new competencies. Absorbing new competencies is only considered effective if they are properly retained by the receiver. Therefore, the relation between emitter and recipient relies on the strength of communication channels as well as trust.

Table 1.2 summarizes the primary strategic objectives set by members of a strategic alliance.

Theoretical perspective	Strategic objectives
Economic based on transaction costs	Risk sharing
	Rationalize production and economy of scale
	Vertical synergy
	Technological transfer and patent exchange
Strategic-based resource acquisition and dependence	Create value and competitive advantage
	International expansion
	Consolidate strategic position within market
	Combining competencies
	Risk sharing
Organizational learning	Technological and/or patent transfer
	International expansion

Table 1.2. *Theoretical table of objectives leading to a strategic alliance*

1.2. Asymmetric alliances

1.2.1. *Definition*

Symmetry can be explained as a harmonious successive relation where elements are arranged in regularity and balance. In this sense, a strategic alliance is symmetrical when it involves "companies whose strategic positions are interchangeable, meaning companies with comparable levels of resources, competencies and that are at similar stages of development in the race for innovation and the creation of new technologies" [ASS 10, p. 113]. Alliances are considered symmetric when they involve companies of similar sizes and resource levels that operate in geographic areas of similar levels of development [MOU 05].

The negating prefix "a" denies this idea of balance in terms of scale, resources or even experience among partners. Therefore, "asymmetric alliances involve companies with differing strategic positions, in the sense of technological mastery" [ASS 10]. They involve companies with dissimilar sizes, resources and experience that are located in geographical areas of unequal levels of development.

In the following sections, we will detail the organizational, strategic, managerial, geographic and sociocultural factors of asymmetric alliances.

1.2.2. *Criteria for organizational and strategic asymmetry*

1.2.2.1. *Size*

Size constitutes a fundamental factor in the perception of asymmetry within an alliance. The notion of asymmetry can be determined through differences in size, revenue, etc., often indicating differences in structure, cultures, norms or values [MOU 05]. In this respect, size asymmetry between the members of a strategic alliance leads to, in most cases, the risk of unilateral dependence and even opportunism from the dominating party. Using the results from an empirical study involving 344 Small and Medium Enterprises (SME) in the biotechnology sector, Vidot-Delerue and Simon [VID 05] conclude that asymmetry has a heavy impact on the smaller partner's perceived risk of being absorbed by the larger party, which tends to encourage opportunistic behavior. Size asymmetry tends, in most cases, to reinforce the dominant ally's bureaucratic control over the alliance.

1.2.2.2. *Nature and specificity of dedicated resources*

An alliance is asymmetric when it joins partners who supply substantially different resources, whether they be tangible (human, financial, material, infrastructure, etc.) or intangible (informational resources, expertise, notoriety, etc.). Pooling resources creates a mutual dependence among partners. The rarity and specificity of a resource leads to a situation of dependency for its holder over the partner [WIL 85]. The level of dependence among partners will depend on the value of the dedicated resources (whether or not they can be considered strategic) and their availability [YAN 94]. Resources supplied by a host partner in terms of key knowledge pertaining to the local market hold strategic value to a foreign partner. The Multinational Corporation (MNC) then remains dependent upon the local ally until completely internalizing and appropriating all transferred knowledge. Command of a particular skill or craft or experience with the local environment can, most often, constitute a source of power for the host partner who still remains reliant on the transfer of technological expertise and skills from the MNC.

1.2.2.3. Level of experience

The level of experience manifests through the ability for partners to manage organizational interactions and conflict [HAR 85]. The company that has a lot of experience with collaborations, expertise, technological abilities, managerial and organizational skills is expected to use its assets to benefit its partner. Power dynamics then set in and we start to see asymmetric dependence within the partnership. The company with the least amount of experience benefits from the abilities and knowledge from its partner at a far lower cost than would be possible at market rate, but will see its power and autonomy toward its partner reduce.

1.2.2.4. Learning and absorptive capacities

The dominant partner's absorptive capacity (a global corporation, for example) is generally higher than the dominated one's (an SME for example) [O'DW 05]. This way, transfers of knowledge are greater between companies in a symmetrical *alliance* than in asymmetric alliances. In asymmetric alliances, the dominant party, having the most abilities, will, in most cases, determine the governance model in the relationship as well as the nature of the knowledge that is transferred to the host partner. The knowledge transfer will not only rely on the will of the partner to learn, but also its absorptive capacity [COH 90].

1.2.3. *Criteria for managerial asymmetry: the governance model*

There is a strong correlation between one partner's power and size. The dominant partner naturally possesses significant human, financial and technological assets, which contributes to reinforcing the power imbalance in the alliance [CHR 05, LU 06, MEI 10]. Size asymmetry among partners explains the asymmetry in governance of the alliance with disparities in the way each party is represented in the capital structure (majority holder versus minority holder) and management style (dominant versus submissive). And yet, power asymmetry cannot be exclusively the consequence of the ownership structure of the alliance, as there are other asymmetry criteria such as the nature and specificity of resources supplied by the parties. In the case of an alliance, information withholding can affect the progress of joint activities, although sharing information can often give alliance members the impression that they are losing power and control over the partnership.

Agency theory [JEN 76] introduces the notion of information asymmetry and emphasizes the issue of imperfect information and opportunistic behaviors inherent to conflicts of interest, which inevitably translate to "agency costs" among the members of a contractual relationship.

We distinguish between two contexts for information asymmetry between the partners in an asymmetric alliance:

1) a context of adverse selection, particularly if the host partner does not have the technical and organizational knowledge that the international partner does, while the latter is not familiar with the local environment;

2) a context of moral hazard, knowing that either partner can change their behavior according to their environment and strategy.

The notion of " information power" refers to "the ability for an economic agent to modifier, through direct or indirect action, the behavior, conditions or economic results of other units in order to secure a financial advantage" [GUI 04, p. 10]. This power will depend on a certain number of variables tied to the level of information asymmetry as well as the specificity of actors relative to their rationality or their choices and personal interests.

1.2.4. Geographic and sociocultural asymmetry criteria

1.2.4.1. Geographic origin

The asymmetric aspect of a strategic alliance can be the result of differences in geographic origins of partner companies [CHR 05]. According to Mouline [MOU 05], there are two types of cataloged international strategic alliances depending on geographic criteria: classic alliances established between developed countries, North–North alliances, and North–South alliances, which involve both developed and developing countries, such as asymmetric alliances established between European or American companies and Asian companies (excluding Japan). These different agreements are set apart by different objectives for partners, organization models, length of agreement, governance model or even perceived importance of the alliance for each partner [HYD 99, TIN 05].

The result is differences in governance structures and conflict resolution models used by the partners within each type of alliance [HYD 99]. While disagreements of a strategic nature arising in North–North alliances are solved in a formal manner with contract clauses, it should be noted that North–South alliances are more often faced with divergences of a tactical and operational nature requiring they resort to conflict resolution mechanisms that are more or less informal.

1.2.4.2. *Culture*

Cultural proximity among partners is considered to be a factor of trust within alliances that favors mutual understanding [INK 04]. Locating activities in countries that are culturally close increases the chances of success of the alliance [DRO 06]. However, cultural distance refers to cultural and organizational differences among the members of an alliance [PAR 93]. This refers to existing differences between national cultures, organizational processes and managerial behaviors of partners. The cultural distance among partners is a source of ambiguity and managerial complexity which impedes the convergence of their objectives [DOZ 88].

A number of studies highlight the failures of alliances as a result of cultural distance between partners that translates to differences in histories, vision, behaviors, managerial styles or even decision-making methods within the alliance [BLA 06]. A large cultural distance between partners can lead to incompatibilities in their organizational and administrative operation impacting the way they approach and solve the difficulties they are faced with [KOG 88]. These divergences can create an atmosphere of uncertainty and defiance leading to elevated coordination and supervision costs. Transactions concluded among culturally different partners can translate to an inability to predict future results, increasing uncertainty and amplifying coordination costs. Any such situation, characterized by a lack of trust, requires more prevention against opportunism, thus explaining increased transaction costs.

Table 1.3 collates the criteria for asymmetry that have been cited previously.

Factors		Reference
Organizational and strategic factors	Size	[HAR 85] [BEA 05] [MOU 05] [TIN 05] [VID 05]
	Nature and specificity of supplied resources	[YAN 94] [YAN 98] [INK 97] [LEE 03] [CHR 05]
	Level of experience	[HAR 85] [MOU 05]
Managerial factors	Learning and absorptive capacity	[INK 97] [O'DW 05]
	Governance model	[LEC 84] [YAN 94] [LEE 03] [CHR 05] [O'DW 05]
	Level of information sharing	[MOH 94] [VID 05]
Sociocultural and geographic factors	Geographic origin	[CHR 05] [MOU 05] [MAK 98]
	Culture	[PAR 91, PAR 93] [KOG 88] [SIM 99] [SAR 01]

Table 1.3. *Asymmetry factors in strategic alliances*

2

Management Specificities of North and South Asymmetric Alliances

2.1. Definition

North and South strategic alliances are asymmetric alliances considering that the terms "North" and "South" do not necessarily refer to a geographic reality, but generally represent an economic approach that tends to consider that "Northern" countries generally dispose of higher levels of resources, capital, industrialization and generated wealth than "Southern" countries [SUR 09]. This asymmetry can be both qualitative and quantitative pertaining to the nature and level of reputation of companies, the value and variety of their portfolio of knowledge and abilities or even the level of economic development of their country of origin.

2.2. Organizational form

The partners' choice of organizational form for their alliance depends on a number of criteria, in particular their set objectives, the desired amount of independence vis-à-vis their partner, the extent of the collaboration, the way they wish to approach and anticipate risks of opportunism or even the legal restrictions that regulate the political, economic or legal environment of the alliance. Pisano [PIS 89] cites the theory of transaction costs to highlight the fact that the governance structures of a strategic alliance include equity-based alliances relying on joint investments and joint ventures as well as non-equity-based alliances, the choice of which depends on the level of uncertainty of the environment and the specificity of the assets.

Using the network approach as a basis, Chen and Chen [CHE 02] state that the level of commitment of resources and organizational integration that characterize the partners constitutes the deciding choice of the organizational form of a strategic alliance. Using a study involving 1,597 local Taiwanese companies, the authors conclude that these companies tend to engage in strategic alliances with global corporations in order to use their resources, improve their capacities or even access new markets. Equity-based alliances prove to be particularly interesting for large-scale companies allowing them to mobilize financial and human resources specifically to the alliance. However, smaller companies generally having limited financial resources cannot easily fragment their operational resources and affect them to an equity alliance. It should be noted that the higher the level of interdependence between partners, the more they are committed and involved in the alliance, making potential exit costs higher.

The creation of a joint venture allows companies to face the uncertainties of the competitive environment by granting a certain autonomy to the host partner to adapt to the specificities of its market. Equity ownership is a key part of the joint venture allowing the alignment of objectives, and thus reducing the risk of opportunistic behavior of partners. North and South alliances tend to be long term, taking the form of a joint subsidiary or a long-term supply agreement [MOU 05]. Yet, the choice of a joint venture as a development model in an emerging country is likely to lead to various categories of risk [JOL 01]. The imbalance linked to the geographic coverage of partners can emphasize the asymmetry of the alliance and generate tension or even conflict.

Using the example of the Sino-foreign joint venture Danone Wahaha established in 1996, Joly [JOL 01] highlights the exogenous and endogenous risks associated with a joint venture. Thus, the risks are tied to the two Western and Chinese management models as well as to the cultural distances, the risk of opportunistic behavior, in particular non-compliance with contract clauses by the host partner or appropriation of expertise from the Multinational Corporation (MNC) in order to use it outside of the alliance (risk of product counterfeiting (risk of imitation, copy without the consent of the MNC/MNC), or even the risk of a takeover of one of the partners by the other). Exogenous risks, on the other hand, relate to changes in public policy (tax conditions local restrictions). Lastly, the author states that there are risks shared by both parties, which relate to the project itself.

Companies from developed countries having contracted an asymmetric alliance tend, in general, to transfer only a few simple peripheral activities to the host partner, setting certain restrictions as to the use of their expertise, thus protecting their technological capacity, in the absence, in most cases, of any proper legal framework for the protection of intellectual rights.

2.3. Strategic objectives of partners

Compared with Northern companies, Southern companies tend to have insufficient resources, in particular in terms of technological and financial assets. Strategic alliances with countries from developing countries therefore become strategic leverage allowing companies to acquire the resources they lack and access managerial and technical abilities allowing them to reinforce their competitive position. As for

"Northern" corporations, they are looking for a "Southern" partner able to help them control the specificities of the market they are trying to enter while reinforcing their competitive advantage by benefiting from low production costs of emerging nations. Internalizing activity generates adjustment costs due to local restrictions (local legislations and practices), which tend to be higher when differentiation imperatives (that means that the local market presents a set of specificities due to the preferences of the consumer, which are very different from the preferences and characteristics of the MNC) are high on the new market.

North and South alliances can thus be justified by the transaction costs approach according to which Northern companies enter partnerships with Southern companies in order to minimize production costs, in particular in terms of workforce costs. Strategic alliances therefore allow gains in economy of scale. They also grant Northern companies greater control over resources and markets as well as an increased diversity that allows them to compensate for maturing or declining sales of certain products. In other words, an alliance can be created in order to extend the perimeter of the organization, benefit from growth opportunities and spread risk on a global scale [JEA 14]. These assets grant Northern companies additional financial power allowing them to finance important R&D expenses.

Using the resource-based view [HAM 94], North–South alliances respond to the necessity to combine new abilities, particularly industrial ones, or the need to explore new markets and learn about the industrial structures of target countries [HYD 99]. By entering a strategic alliance, the Northern country can benefit from its technological investments by transferring its products reaching maturity to an emerging country. The objective of the transfer is to prolong the lifecycle of products while maintaining state-of-the-art products in their original markets. Meanwhile, the

Southern company can, through the alliance, develop new abilities and skills, and expand its activities, thus creating new sources of competitive advantage [BEL 01].

Looking at the typology of the motivations driving collaborations as identified by Contractor and Lorange [CON 88], we can highlight the fact that strategic alliances grants Southern companies with opportunities to benefit from new competencies, knowledge, expertise and abilities that are crucial to reinforcing their competitiveness. This, in turn, allows them to experience greater credibility toward their environment and particularly in the eyes of their clients. The choice of an alliance strategy fits into a dynamic of organizational learning and access to new resources, in particular technological ones [YAN 14, MIT 00] associated with both the design and the production of new products. By associating with their Northern partners, Southern companies have the possibility to acquire new expertise and knowledge susceptible to help them in overcoming their technological deficiencies. Nonetheless, the elements that tend to get transferred are generally tied to technological support, for example management methods and production processes rather than actual technology.

We note that the partners within an asymmetric alliance often have expectations that differ from the final results of the operation [DOZ 88]. Their objectives in terms of financial performance, market shares or even technological and managerial integration vary from one partner to another. Incompatibilities in objectives among partners can cause dysfunction and conflict as a result of withheld information or distortions, which can lead to the overall failure of the collaboration [BUC 93]. Thus, the cultural compatibility in terms of norms, values, symbols and shared expectations potentially inducing compatible behaviors among partners constitutes a crucial element in the competence transfer process of an asymmetric alliance.

2.4. Nature of pooled resources

North–South alliances are generally characterized by uneven contributions from partners, with most cases seeing a unilateral equity investment by the Northern partner that agrees to assist its local counterpart in catching up its strategic, technological and managerial capacities [BEL 01]. The dedicated resources and assets are asymmetric both in a qualitative and a quantitative capacity. These include financial and human resources, management tools and practices, transferred via expatriate staff dedicated to the alliance, or through managerial practices and methods associated with specific organizational cultures.

The resources committed by the Northern partner include, most often, resources that are technological and financial in nature, its brand recognition, managerial and organizational skills, etc. However, the resources shared by the Southern partner include knowledge of the institutional and sociopolitical context, the specificities of local markets (consumer behaviors, market structures, networks of suppliers and distributors as well as finance processes and other proposed tax incentives), or even the ability to enhance their partner's image and brand on the local market [MIL 96]. An initially imbalanced and asymmetric investment within the value chain thus creates a growing dependence of the local firm toward their MNC.

North–South strategic alliances are also distinguished by an asymmetry in the portfolio of knowledge and abilities of each partner. This imbalance in terms of strategic assets and key competences can justify reservations on the behalf of the Northern partner, in sharing its knowledge, out of fear of opportunistic behavior from the host partner (risk of the alliance splitting after competences have been transferred and once the local company has ensured it has overcome its technological deficiencies).

Furthermore, cultural distance between partners can complicate the knowledge transfer process and be the cause of the alliance failing [SIM 04]. Spatial, temporal and linguistic distances between partners are likely to amplify difficulties in learning and transferring new skills [CHR 05].

Taking these restrictions into consideration, the dominant partner will be inclined to minimize the transfer of new abilities in order to reduce the chances of the smaller partner appropriating its key abilities with no counterpart [DAS 99] by putting in place surreptitious ways to impede information and ability acquisitions. Beyond the risks of appropriation of its knowledge, the larger partner also runs a risk related to the smaller company's opportunism, which can unilaterally decide to end the cooperation once it has reached its objectives and compensated its deficiencies.

2.5. Managerial system and control mechanisms

Control plays a central role in the governance of asymmetric strategic alliances in terms of reducing risks of opportunistic behaviors [PAR 93]. Strategic alliances are exposed to a large amount of uncertainty leading companies and individuals from different locations to work together toward divergent objectives with their disadvantage being a limited knowledge of the environment and market within which they are trying to establish themselves. In addition, the arbitration between accomplishing objectives and reducing risks is, in itself, a complex task, particularly when it involves numerous partners from different nationalities and cultures as are the case with North and South alliances. Thus, the complexity of the organizational structure of these types of alliances, paired with the risk of deviating and opportunistic behaviors by other partners, force the latter to monitor one another.

Operational control of a joint venture established by two asymmetric partners, characterized by specific visions, managerial practices and cultures, often presents the challenge of power distribution within the alliance. The structure of the control within an asymmetric alliance depends on a number of attributes such as the size of alliance members, their competitive positions, the variety of their products and resources [CHE 02]. The dedicated resources represent an important factor when allocating capital, determining the control structure and during negotiations between partners [YAN 94, YAN 98, INK 97]. The negotiating power relates to the contributions of each member of the alliance and depends on the type of provided resources (tangible/intangible) as well as their level of dependency [PFE 78]. Thus, the heterogeneousness of resources impacts the control structure of the alliance, leading to partners opting for an asymmetric governance structure.

The governance model of the alliance reflects the power relation within the alliance, the latter being dependent on the respective contributions of each partner. Thus, the negotiating power of each member within a joint venture will depend on the resources committed to the project rather than the distribution of capital [MJO 97]. The partner that has the stronger position due to the resources it provides is likely to dictate the conditions of the agreement surrounding the alliance to its host partner, making the latter even more dependent on the former. The level of asymmetry among partners not only determines the distribution of negotiating power and internal power dynamics [CHE 14] but also impacts the trust within the relationship. The level of formal control imposed by the more powerful partner over its local counterpart will therefore be higher when there is a large asymmetry between partners.

If there is little asymmetry, partners can rely on their relational capital based on mutual trust to govern the joint activities, while preferring control mechanisms established by contract where asymmetry is high [VID 05]. Trust remains an important factor in the governance of the alliance, regardless of the level of asymmetry between partners. It should be noted that the environmental context is likely to influence the governance structure of the asymmetric alliance [LEC 84, LEE 03]. In certain cases, the MNC can be obliged to assume a minority position in the joint venture as a result of restrictive regulations in the local country. The former can then control activities with high added value or maintain operational control over joint activities.

The dominant company tends to control the strategic functions of the joint subsidiary, while the host partner maintains operational control. The separation between activities surrounding strategic and operational control will depend, once again, on the nature of the committed resources of each partner, which, while not controlling the entirety of local joint activity, will at least control the use of the resources they provided to the alliance.

3

Alliance Governance by IS

3.1. Information systems (IS)

3.1.1. *Definition*

The concept of an information system can be defined as a formalized device that receives, processes, stores, manipulates and communicates flows of information that, coupled with technological tools, are used to assist processes of decision making, coordination and collective or individual control within one or more organizations. Andreu *et al.* [AND 92], Alter [ALT 96], Reix *et al.* [REI 11, p. 67] highlight, in this regard, the importance of coherently combining and articulating resources (materials, software, personnel, data, procedures) allowing for data acquisition, processing and storage. Information systems appear as an important tool for transaction processes, decision making and inter- or intraorganization communications [KEF 10].

3.1.2. *Possible applications*

IS are generally grouped into three distinct themes of applications, which will be presented in the following sections.

3.1.2.1. *Operational applications*

These are functional IS that support transaction and operation processing and assist in conveying information useful for management. Functional systems allow for the management of four specific functions within the organization: the trade and marketing function, the production function, the accounting and finance function and the human resources function. It is, nonetheless, important to maintain organizational coherence, something based on the communication of joint representations and the use of unique frameworks through the use of databases or an Enterprise Resource Planning (ERP):

– The use of a database allows companies to manage information in a global and singular way [DEL 08]. The need to conceive information in a global fashion, organize it and distribute it to the various operators leads to the development of common frameworks known as data repositories. In this way, a human resources data repository, for example, will hold all information surrounding salary payment operations, workforce attendance times, recruitment, career progression, training, assessment reports, etc. The point is to collect, for each employee, information surrounding his or her personal characteristics, career path, professional abilities, job sheet, or even his or her salary and the tasks he/she has been assigned by the company. The systemization of complex analysis of this information, thanks to databases, helps reduce data entry operations into multiple systems that can be costly and prone to error. In a client database, the repository will list all information pertaining to each client and define the link between each of these clients and other information in the database (their orders, products ordered that are representative of what the company has been dealing with, etc.).

The disadvantage for a company to have to maintain separate databases to manage its different functions lies in the complexity of internal data exchanges. The latter exist in different and often incompatible formats, requiring manual manipulations to successfully extract information from various systems, to standardize, process and present it in a comprehensible and usable format.

– Integrated management software packages offer a modular architecture (trade management, accountancy, production management, etc.) organized around a central database that manages the entirety of the organization's information. Operational information is stored in the database and communicates with all surrounding modules using automated processes configured by the user. The main developers of ERP are SAP notably (SAP R/3) since 1993, PeopleSoft, Oracle, Microsoft, Sage, JD Edwards.

The advantage of an ERP when compared to other integrated software solutions is in its level of integration, since practically every function is included, with the exception of certain specific functions that operate on a non-formalized routine such as R&D. According to the principle of integration, each datum exists only in one location of the database. Each fragment of data is therefore standardized making it easier to access the entirety or a subset of data depending on one's needs. For instance, the production service can easily look-up sales previsions for the marketing department and view the calculated actual costs by the accountancy department. It therefore becomes easy to access a global view of the financial viability of the company by simply and efficiently compiling all of this accessible information. This integrated view of the data, coupled with the potential of Internet technology, grants members of the company access to all the information they need, regardless of their geographic location. Because of a standardized web interface to which they have access, members can reach the information required to perform their duties. This web interface is referred to as an "intranet" and allows members of an organization to access its data through web technologies.

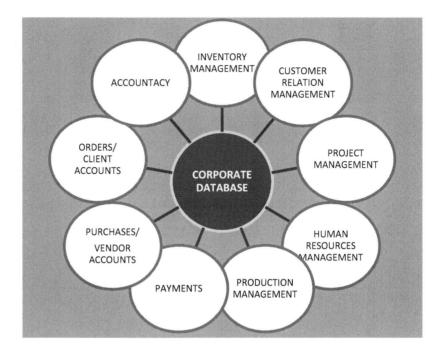

Figure 3.1. *Layout of an integrated software package*

3.1.2.2. *Decision support applications*

Decision support applications include interactive systems that assist in decision-making processes, on the one hand, and knowledge management, on the other hand:

– Decision support software (DSS) or decision-making software as well and Business Intelligence applications collate data from other application systems from various Data Warehouses for multidimensional analyses in order to produce control panels and indexes that support decision-making operations. DSS assist decision makers through their ability to:

- collect, integrate, summarize and transform the operational data of an IS;

- appropriately memorize decision-related data;

- process these data (updates, precalculations);

- present this information in a way that facilitates decision making.

Decision support information systems must provide the tools necessary to allow companies to execute the governance models defined by management. The point is to collect and organize operational information and then present and broadcast it using reporting systems and normalized control panels.

– Knowledge management applications: Companies are increasingly concerned with the digital management of their accumulated knowledge. Knowledge is becoming one of the most precious assets for companies. Note that knowledge should not be confused with information and data. Data are millions of raw facts conveyed by operational systems. Information is a collection of data that make sense within a defined context. Knowledge, however, can be defined as information that has been assimilated by operators, leading to skills or expertise that are reusable in the operation and development of activities.

Information and communication technologies (ICT) play an essential role in knowledge management by enabling its extraction, structuring, capitalization, distribution or even its use. According to Crié [CRI 03, p. 45], "technology makes it easier to formalize intelligence and the experience of individuals in order to grant access to the right information to the right person and at the right time". In this context, we can use the works of Charlot and Lancini [CHA 04] to distinguish between two large categories of knowledge management IS applications: integrated software for capitalization and interactive software for knowledge distribution. While the former category of software are used to process, reuse and broadcast knowledge, the latter are designed to support collaboration by encouraging exchanges and the creation of new knowledge.

3.1.2.3. *Communication support applications*

Technologies used in communication processes are extremely varied, encompassing interorganizational information sharing systems (IOISS) and the use of the Internet. In this sense, e-mail is the most ubiquitous among these Internet technologies for facilitating data exchanges (administrative files, meeting schedules), providing information and technical documents (procedure guidelines, activity reports, meeting transcripts, documentation search engines, agendas, Internet portals, etc.).

Field of application of an information system	Role of the information system	Examples of applications
Operational applications	Collect, memorize and process data necessary to conducting activities. Digitize and optimize operational information.	Purchasing, inventory, logistics, production management, sales monitoring, payments, workflow.
Decision support applications	Provide relevant indicators surrounding company activity assisting analysis and decision making. Increase partners' knowledge (suppliers, clients, vendors, etc.) Formalize, promote and distribute knowledge.	Client database, purchase history, CRM, control panels, reporting.
Communication support applications	Communicate information internally and externally.	Messaging, groupware, EDI, supply chain, extranet, intranet, Internet.

Table 3.1. *Classification of information systems software*

The progress of technologies allowing for the exchanges of information between different organizations leads to the creation of veritable networks of partners that regularly partake in transactional or collaborative relations. This phenomenon has multiple consequences on a strategic level (choice of partners), an organizational level (control and coordination modalities) and on the development of information systems necessary for sustaining collaborations with partners.

3.2. Interorganizational information systems (IOIS)

3.2.1. *Definition*

Historically, the notion of IS is closely linked to internal company information. The first applications to be developed focused on specific activities such as fracking, accounting, etc. Information and communication technologies then came and connected and integrated different activities within companies, thus improving internal coordination. Interorganizational integration was the result of a need to improve communications and the conditions for exchanges of information between different organizations. Table 3.1 summarizes the primary definitions of IOIS.

Definition	References
Interorganizational systems (IOS) are defined as automated information systems shared by two or more companies.	[CAS 85]
A system through which two or more independently managed organizations communicate within a company, cooperative or commercial network, memory to memory, with no physical means of transfer, by exchanging data, e-mail or external database applications.	[SUO 91]
A collection of materials, software, data and procedures that support the automated exchange of information between two distinct organizations.	[REI 02]
Information systems that automate the flow of information across organizational boundaries and link a company to its customers, distributors or suppliers.	[LAU 15]

Table 3.2. *Definitions for interorganizational information systems*

3.2.2. *Possible applications for IOIS*

It is possible to define three distinct categories of IOIS based on their functional characteristics:

– request-based IOIS: these are shared IOIS that allow users to consult databases such are shared databases, a shared extranet or electronic marketplaces. The exchange of electronic data involves no legal restrictions for the participating organizations. Security restrictions are reduced *de facto* and the uses for the data can be varied. The only standardization is the consulting procedure;

– transaction-based IOIS: these are value-chain type IOIS designed to manage the data linked to a transaction. The exchange of digital data is fundamental to this type of IOIS, most often supported by Electronic Data Interchange (EDI). This is a computer program used to send and receive commercial forms. The advantage of this technology lies in its interoperability. As stated by Vernadat [VER 09], interoperability must first overcome organizational barriers, and, second, improve interactions between systems, users, departments and companies (in terms of flow of matter, flow of information and decision-making flows). Areas of application covered by ED mostly correspond to transactional uses or commercial uses. The normalization of electronic documents guarantees the reliability of transactions. In this type of system, objectives among partners are complementary and cost sharing is easy. The IOIS is managed by the client, the supplier or a collective of clients or suppliers.

– Partners exchanging electronic data over the Internet must use security measures to protect their data. Another limitation is the standard formats that must be used in particular for any company dealing with partners across industries and located in different parts of the globe. Rather than using a traditional EDI, said company may then elect to use widely accessible programs, such as XML, to transmit documents over the Internet. This method considerably reduces the cost of exchanging electronic documents from system to system as a result of an initial investment and reduced network usage costs;

– task-support IOIS: this type of IOIS corresponds to situations of cooperative work between different organizations. These are groupware type collaboration tools and video conferences as well as e-mail, chat applications and online phoning (Skype for example). According to Courbon and Tajan [COU 99], groupwares can be defined as the technologies and associative work methods that, through the intermediary of electronic communications, allow users to share information over a digital platform to a group engaging in a collaboration. These technologies encourage remote collaboration by enabling parties to share information and interact. They also reduce the inherent problems that come with geographic distance between partners and asynchronous work.

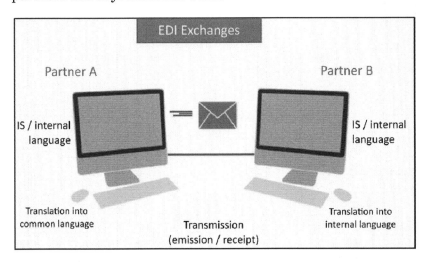

Figure 3.2. *Presentation of an EDI*

Field of application of IOIS	Role of the IOIS	Configuration of the IOIS	Examples
Request-based IOIS	Consulting databases		Electronic marketplaces Database sharing Extranet
Transaction-based IOIS	Automation of messages pertaining to transactions		EDI transaction systems XML transaction systems
Task-support IOIS	Support collaborative work between organizations		Video conferences Screen sharing

Table 3.3. *Classification of interorganizational information systems programs (adapted from [KUM 96])*

3.3. Analysis of the role of IS in the management of strategic alliances

Companies engaging in strategic alliances support high transaction costs. They are most often exposed to the risk of opportunism from their partners and of limited rationality generated by the unpredictable nature of the environment. This makes it impossible for them to assess and accurately predict their partners' inputs, objectives and behaviors especially when there is large geographic distance between them. In addition, problems relating to informational asymmetry are susceptible to impeding processes of control and assessment of the alliance performance. This means that it is nowadays impossible to consider control strategies for alliances without the integration of an IS, which will support both formal and informal mechanisms.

3.3.1. *Formal governance tool*

Formal mechanisms refer to a collection of standards, codified rules and procedures that allow for the realization of common objectives [DAS 98]. We can distinguish between various formal control mechanisms including the standardization of results, direct supervision and standardization of work processes [MIN 79, MAR 89].

The use of information systems supports performance control relying on standardized procedures and the use of reporting tools. Through its capacity to memorize information relating to the work performed by members of the company, the information system increases the efficiency of control devices for its workforce and reduces the need for direct supervision [LEC 13]. IS can therefore increase the transparency and traceability within the organization, monitor individual behaviors and performance and thus reduce the presence of undesirable behaviors. In this context, ERP play a key role in homogenizing IS, standardizing the operation of the organization and enabling the transversal integration of applications and business processes, thus enabling in the same way a better control and organizational governance. Monitoring activity allows them to react quickly to hazards linked to supply or markets and adapt their resources to activity levels [KOC 10].

The introduction of IS enhances, among other things, operational control. Investing in IS allows companies to increase their information processing capacities and automate control, thus contributing toward replacing traditional hierarchic control methods [GAL 74]. The deployment of IS within an organization optimizes central managerial control via the promotion of circumstances where operators' choices and flexibility are largely predetermined.

Other than internal control instruments, the technocratic control instruments based on the use of instrumental artifacts do play an important role in interorganizational relations [HOL 05]. The introduction of information systems assist the control of the results of the alliance and reduce uncertainty, complexity and the risk of opportunistic behaviors from partners [AND 06].

By reducing transactional risks, manipulation errors or informational asymmetry among partners while allowing smooth access to information necessary to making decisions, the use of an information system can significantly increase the performance of an alliance. In the case of asymmetric alliances, the partner in an unfavorable situation of dependency may resort to an information system to attempt to reduce informational asymmetry and gain a better understanding of their ally [DON 05] by creating an atmosphere of trust within the alliance. This means that the use of an information system not only secures exchanges and enables a more solid control of interorganizational relations, but it also reduces the risks of opportunism or non-cooperative behaviors from key players within the alliance.

3.3.2. *Informal governance tool*

Formal control cannot replace informal control that refers to informal communication as well as the creation and development of a common culture [VID 05, ZAH 95]. Therefore, the informal governance of an alliance can be reinforced through socialization mechanisms that help build a common organizational culture either through personal training or the presence of staff assigned to the joint venture. It should be noted that the use of assigned staff within the alliance reinforces communication between partners, helps convey organizational values of the FMN and improve acquisition of knowledge and abilities by local staff [NOH 94]. Thus, face-to-face exchanges of information constitute an essential element in the process of socializing partners. In this vein, Kalika *et al.* [KAL 07] highlight the importance of face-to-face association, video training and/or electronic exchanges in the development of personal relations between members of two organizations as well as in the establishment of a dynamic that encourages the transfer of knowledge among partners.

Communication tools such as the telephone, e-mail, videoconferencing or even electronic exchanges of data improve interactions while simultaneously reducing informational asymmetry between two partners. These exchanges allow members to get to know one-another, they reduce the risks of miscommunications and therefore improve the results of joint tasks [BRI 13]. Information systems help deploy resources and abilities from the company on the scale of different countries, thus encouraging the development of information networks [BHA 13]. The use of IS grants a centralized access to a high volume of information and knowledge, thus encouraging the capitalization of knowledge and the integration strategic abilities by partners.

By relying on information processing mechanisms, partners are able to solve problems of equivocity and environmental uncertainty and therefore more easily construct a shared interpretation and meaning to information [THO 93]. Uncertainty is considered as the result of a lack of information not only through "poor" media, such as written reports, but also via "rich" media such as audiovisual applications.

The choice of an information system then appears as the result of a rational process that must account for and make sense of the objectives set by partners with restrictions resulting from its architecture, content and technical characteristics. By encouraging exchanges of opinions, sentiments and interpretations between partners on the basis of "rich" media [THO 93], the latter is meant to improve exchanges by favoring the control modalities, both strategic and operational, of the joint activity.

The Role of IS in the Management of an Asymmetric Alliance: Four Case Studies

Introduction to Part 2

In order to study the role of IS in the management of asymmetric alliances, we focused primarily on North–South alliances, in particular Euro-Tunisian cases, characterized by important asymmetries in size as well as in resources between partners.

Below, we define the specifics behind the context of our study:

– the number of North–South Mediterranean alliances increased as a result of the creation of a "Euromed" partnership zone in 1976 between various European members and Mediterranean southern companies for various fields of activity as well as the creation of the Barcelona process in 1995. The latter's main objective is the creation of a zone of peace, stability and prosperity along with the gradual introduction of an open-trade zone. In the current context of globalization, this process appears as an alternative for Mediterranean companies. The creation of a number of North–South free-trade agreements and the geographic and cultural proximity between both zones are the reason for the number of researchers that have taken an interest in the exchanges between established and emerging economies [SAÏ 06, CHE 08, DIK 10, CHE 14]. According to data offered by a report from the UNCTAD[1], European investors seem more inclined to invest in Africa, in particular in Northern Africa where investments have increased by 35% reaching 9 billion euros in 2012. The participation by the Tunisian government to GATT-WTO[2] in 1990 remains a logical accomplishment and a step toward greater exposure and diversity for the nation's economy. According to the terms set by article XXIV, paragraph 4 of the agreement, "The contracting parties recognize the desirability of increasing freedom of trade by the development, through voluntary agreements, of closer integration between the economies of the countries parties to such agreements". This decision explains the growing number of strategic partnerships between Tunisia and the EU, in particular with France, which, in 2014, remains Tunisia's primary foreign investor, making up 18% of its overall foreign direct investments (FDI);

– despite a transitioning Tunisian social, political and economic context since the advent of the "Arab Spring" in 2011, the Tunisian government persevered in its efforts to maintain the volume of FDI, stabilize the economic situation, reassure foreign investors that were worried about the political instability, stimulate recover in all sectors and establish civil peace. According to the Foreign Investment Promotion Agency (FIPA)[3], the volume of FDI reached, in 2013, over 900 million euro, which was an increase of 14% compared to 2011. Furthermore, the European Union remains Tunisia's primary economic partner: "78% of exports, 65% of Tunisian imports come from there, it generates 85% of its tourism revenue and ensures 75% of foreign investments in the country" until 2014.

---

1 UNCTAD: United Nations Conference on Trade and Development.

2 GATT-WTO: General Agreement on Tariffs and Trade, World Trade Organization.

3 FIPA: www.investintunisia.tn.

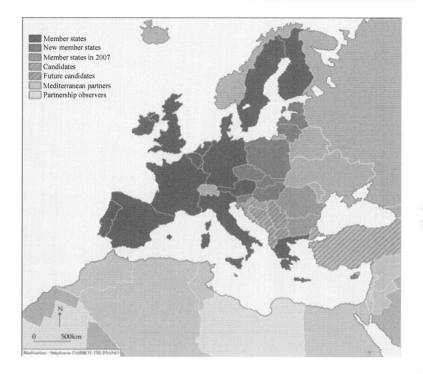

Figure I.1. *The Euro-Mediterranean partnership. For a color version of this figure, see ww.iste.co.uk/said/alliances.zip*

Methodology

Using research based on a qualitative approach, we study four cases of strategic alliances connecting Tunisian and European companies together. These alliances are set in the agribusiness sector (cases cases) and the automotive industry (two cases). The most common form of alliance is the contractual form, which are present in three of the cases and one case of equity-based alliance. The alliances were all created between 1997 and 2010. We performed 31 semidirective interviews with personnel involved in these alliances in order to increase the reliability of the data collected. In this way, we spoke to MDs, R&D directors, IS directors, etc. The total number of hours of interview is near

45, corresponding to a total of 409 pages. We recorded these interviews in order to avoid note-taking and to ensure the collected data was exhaustive and more reliable. The four cases we studied use secondary data on an internal (company documents, screenshots, activity reports) and external level (websites, press excerpts) in the context of an empirical triangulation [YIN 09]. Table I.1 presents a few elements on the study sample.

Case	Field of activity	Alliance form	Creation date	Nationality of the European partner
ALPHA	Agribusiness	Joint venture (50/50)	1997	France
DELTA	Agribusiness	License	2006	France
KAPPA	Automotive	Partnership	2010	France
IOTA	Automotive	Partnership	2002	France

Table I.1. *Sample presentation*

Functions	Tunisian partners	Functions	European partners
	Number		Number
IS director and management control	4	IS director	4
R&D director	2	Marketing director	2
Marketing director	3	Production director	2
Managing director	4	Managing director	3
Deputy CEO	2	R&D director	1
Commercial director	1	Head of IT	1
Project manager	1	Commercial director	1
Total	17	Total	14

Table I.2. *Functions of the respondents*

Case	Number of interviews with the Tunisian partner	Number of interviews with the European partner	Total number of interviews
ALPHA	3	4	7
DELTA	3	3	6
IOTA	4	1	5
KAPPA	4	1	5
Total	17	14	31

Table I.3. *Number of interviews with European and Tunisian partners*

4

Case ALPHA

4.1. Characteristics of alliance ALPHA

4.1.1. *Organizational form of the alliance*

In 1997, the contract of the strategic alliance between ALPHA N and ALPHA S was signed in the form of a joint venture on an equal basis in terms of equity and negotiating power. The deputy CEO of ALPHA N confirms that "In this relationship, there is a positive interaction in both directions (...) it is a co-management where both parties act together to govern a common project".

This relationship starts out with a necessity, particularly for the French partner: to circumvent the reluctance of the CEO of ALPHA S to the creation of an alliance. Sharing power was not an easy task for the owner of a family company, who to this day expresses his concerns with this decision. The managing director of ALPHA S confirms that "The CEO of ALPHA S could not easily give away part of the company that he had himself created and grown, nor accept to share the management of his company". After a lot of hesitation, the CEO of ALPHA S finally accepted the offer from ALPHA N.

This is a strategic alliance created in 1997 under the form of a joint venture with the creation of a jointly held subsidiary divided equally between both strategic partners (50/50) in the agribusiness sector. The jointly created subsidiary was designed to develop, produce and commercialize yoghurts on the Tunisian market.

Partner ALPHA S[1]	Partner ALPHA N[2]
– Tunisian SME created in 1978, local market leader in dairy produce	– French agribusiness group created in 1973, world leader in the production and commercialization of fresh dairy products
– Staff (2011): 654 employees	
– Turnover (2011): 68 millions €	– Staff (2011): 9,000 employees in 400 countries
– ALPHA S uses three base strategies as follows: (1) diversifying in dairy products, maintaining high-added value; (2) maintaining costs; and (3) differentiating products	– Turnover (2011) : 11.02 billion €
	– Two base strategies: recentering and internationalization marked by their presence in developing economies Asia, Central and Eastern Europe, Middle East, Latin America
-- The company produces and distributes three types of products that are complementary in terms of profession, distribution network and strategy: (1) milk and milk-derivate production, (2) fruit juice production, (3) fizzy drinks production. It ensures the distribution of all these products	-- the group is positioned over four strategic areas of activity: (1) fresh dairy products, (2) drinks, (3) children's food and (4) clinical nutrition

Table 4.1. *Presentation of alliance ALPHA[3]*

1 Corresponds to the name we gave the Tunisian company to respect their confidentiality requests.

2 Corresponds to the name we gave the European company to respect their confidentiality requests.

3 The data in Table 4.1 have been collected from institutional websites from two companies that allowed us to get a sense of their activities, their organizations, their missions, etc., beyond the semidirective interviews performed with the two partners of alliance ALPHA between August 2012 and July 2013.

4.1.2. Ends sought by each party

The last decade of the 20th Century was marked by the signing of free-trade agreements between the EU and countries in Northern Africa in an attempt to increase the level of integration of economies characterized with a geographic proximity. During this time, many European companies took an interest in the Tunisian market, in particular its agribusiness sector. More specifically, company ALPHA N expressed the desire to enter the Tunisian market, as it was engaging in internationalization strategies, in order to compete with global leaders in its sector. In a strategic maneuver, ALPHA N looked to create new synergies, conquer market shares and respond to the objective of geographic expansion into the Maghreb: the managing director of ALPHA N confirms that "the objective of ALPHA N consists of reaching a leadership position in the Tunisian market".

On the other hand, the Tunisian company ALPHA S created a strategic alliance with French company ALPHA N in an objective to consolidate its position and competitiveness on the Tunisian market, expand its product range and acquire new skills in the yoghurt industry. The managing director of ALPHA S stated that "It was very interesting for us to partner with ALPHA N as it would allow us to consolidate our position and, more importantly, our viability".

4.1.3. Resources dedicated by both parties

The resources committed by the French partner ALPHA N were both tangible and intangible in nature. During the formation of the alliance, the French partner carried out an in-depth strategic analysis of the local Tunisian company. The Information Systems director at ALPHA N confirmed that "We performed a strategic analysis of our partner's situation". This allowed him to observe the flaws in their information system: The management control and information system director of ALPHA S confirmed that "Our partner found problems in the management process, monetization, cost-analysis, work-methods, data reliability, the nature of the information system in place, etc.". He therefore proposed the nomination of a control and management profile deputy director general in order to refine the IS strategy and the management process of the host partner and increase its performance. The managing director of ALPHA S confirmed that "The partner first proposed the use of an ERP", and continues to say: "Our partner sent a technical director and a deputy CEO, in order to identify and remedy the flaws in our IS. The IS from 1997 has been completely modified by the integration of a JD Edwards type ERP".

Similarly, the resources held by the Tunisian partner ALPHA S are qualified as tangible and intangible, and include infrastructures, premises, human resources, brand notoriety as well as a competitive relational network. As stated by the strategic marketing director of ALPHA N: "The partner ALPHA S has considerable knowledge of the market and possesses a well-developed distribution network". The company ALPHA S is actually the leader on the local market of dairy products. Its sterling reputation and its brand image on the market represented an asset for ALPHA N. The French partner also benefitted from ALPHA S' qualified and competent human resources: The deputy CEO of ALPHA N considers that "The CEO of ALPHA S provides a wealth of knowledge to ALPHA N. What's more, the brand of products ALPHA S is strong and represents a driving force for ours. Associating both brands is clearly an asset for ALPHA N".

In sum, the Tunisian partner possesses a large capital base, which can cover the financial costs incurred during the development phase. The IS and management control director of ALPHA S confirms that "The progress of the alliance over the course of the first four years was characterized by heavy financial investments in order to improve the management process and the growth of our company". The deputy CEO of ALPHA S confirmed that "At first, the company did not make much money, because we emphasized the investment phase" then going on to say: "We started off by reviewing our management. We then engaged our investment focused phase, followed by the launch of the product".

It is important to note the presence of skill transfer within this alliance. The deputy CEO of ALPHA N considers that "In this relationship, there is a positive interaction in both directions". The French partner proceeds to multiple knowledge and expertise transfers in favor of the Tunisian company that internalizes them in order to improve its performance. The deputy CEO of ALPHA N specified that "Marketing is a key point on which we supply our expertise, which makes our partnership function efficiently".

Resources supplied	
Tunisian company ALPHA S	European company ALPHA N
− A strong position on the potential market	− Important skills and expertise in the area of R&D, production processes, marketing
− Infrastructure and premises	− A high-level name and reputation
− Large financial support	− A competitive relational network
− Deep technological legacy	
− A local distribution network	

Table 4.2. *Resources supplied by the partners of the alliance ALPHA*

The Tunisian company improves the transfer of knowledge linked to the market and local consumption habits in favor of the MNC. The strategic marketing director of ALPHA N states that "The CEO of ALPHA S built a strong legacy and a thoroughly developed distribution network because of an in-depth knowledge of the Tunisian market", who then states: "The Tunisian side ensures the alliance's stability when taking strategic decisions while the foreign side ensures the momentum and innovation, in particular with the arrival of new foreign staff and new deputy CEOs".

4.1.4. Perimeter of activity of the alliance

The perimeter of this alliance is large and covers a number of primary and support activities for the value chain. On the marketing side, ALPHA N put in place a new marketing policy based on the definition of advertising campaigns, improved product packaging and broadening the product portfolio. In that vein, the strategic marketing director of ALPHA N states that: "From a marketing aspect, we try to apply the best practices by defining the best packaging, the best publicity messages, etc.". To reach these objectives, the company nominated a strategic marketing deputy CEO: "this deputy CEO was very interested in innovation, in plans of action for increasing sales and improving our position on the market, launching new products, etc.", stated the management control and information system director at ALPHA S.

On a managerial level, ALPHA N created a new management policy for human resources. On a technical level, the company contributed to improving productivity and production processes for the Tunisian partner because of the use of manufacturing processes. The managing director of ALPHA S confirmed "The activity of milk production is exclusively Tunisian, but the positive circumstances that relate to our alliance with ALPHA N lead us to extrapolate our partnership onto this activity. I think this is indicative of our success". From a supply perspective, new knowledge in terms of suppliers and improvements in raw materials was shared.

At a commercial level, "The group is currently the leader in dairy products with 65% of market shares thanks to our alliance with ALPHA N" explains the managing director of ALPHA S who states: "Our objective is to reinforce our strategic position and develop fresh products on the Tunisian market". "The most remarkable evolution is the increase in our revenue and market shares. It's a positive evolution, extremely positive for both parties", explains the managing director of ALPHA N.

1	Conception
2	Development
3	Production
4	Marketing
5	Commercialization

Table 4.3. *The perimeter of the alliance*

4.1.5. *Governance model for the alliance*

To succeed in governing their project, the partners of this strategic alliance started off by signing an agreement on the frequency and modalities of control. First, the transmission of a periodic activity report on a number of key indicators such as revenue, production volume, financial status, etc. As explained by management control and information system director of ALPHA S: "At d+4 of every month, we establish a report, even though we are not consolidated. We also send out Semestrial and Annual reports". The transmission of activity reports occurs following a model predefined by the MNC to avoid difficulties that come with representation, processing and interpreting heterogeneous data. This standardization responds to a need for integration on the French partner's behalf with the objective of comparing information, correlating actions and synchronizing data.

At an organizational level, the partners put in place an administrative board that included both Tunisian and French members. On the Tunisian side, the members involved in this alliance are the CEO, the director of Administration and Finance, the general manager and the management control and information system director. On the French side, the deputy CEO and the management control and information system director and the Middle East and North Africa director are the representatives.

Decision making within this alliance is centralized. The Tunisian company ALPHA S requested equal equity participation in order to be a part of all managerial, technical and strategic decisions. The management control and information systems director at ALPHA S explains: "Our CEO ensured he was part of the decision-making process, for matters such as human resources, without needing to consult with ALPHA N to nominate a new director, for instance, or increase wages". In a similar vein, the managing director of ALPHA S adds: "ALPHA N is ready to pay for everything to obtain full control over the joint subsidiary (...). The final decision always comes down to our CEO who can choose whether or not to accept their proposition".

This way, the governance of the alliance is characterized by mutual participation of both partners with local superiority. The marketing director, the management control and information systems director and the director of Administration and Finance on the Tunisian side are in contact with the foreign deputy CEO who reports all the results from the previous month and the plans of action for upcoming months to the CEO, in order to get his approval: "The deputy CEO is the one who coordinates between ALPHA S and ALPHA N thanks to frequent communications with the CEO. He is the spokesperson", confirms the general manager of ALPHA S.

The strategic partners also take part in phone conferences once a month with the finance director at ALPHA S, the management control and IS director of ALPHA S, the deputy CEO of ALPHA N, marketing director of ALPHA N Middle East and North Africa director. For this conference, the Tunisian partners will consolidate a reporting file following a template defined by the French partners which contains "the current month's results, upcoming plans of action, comments, performance of each direction, cost management levels, problems encountered...", explains the management control and information systems director of ALPHA S.

Verification is carried out via the presence of expatriate staff on site at ALPHA S to organize project reviews. More specifically, "The supervisors for the area perform two visits per year. The first visit at the end of the year to organize the administrative board and the general assembly. The second review to prepare the budget for the following year and revisit the estimations of the ongoing one", states the management control and information systems director on the Tunisian side.

Furthermore, the French company is authorized to perform internal and external audits on the Tunisian company by calling upon auditors with strong international experience. As indicated by the IS management of ALPHA N: "This is a physical audit performed in a preventive capacity rather than a remedial one". However, this audit has only ever been performed once during the startup of the alliance in 1997 in order to assess the situation at ALPHA S and establish its strengths and weaknesses.

The governance of the alliance is not only performed using strict and formal control mechanisms, but also with a permanent and regular monitoring program that grants the French partner a better understanding of the local Tunisian situation. "Our company takes on the role of support and assistance for ALPHA S to help improve its performance", states, in this regard, the deputy CEO of ALPHA N. The presence of expatriate staff from ALPHA N on the site of the host partner contributes to the acquisition of new knowledge from Tunisian personnel by training and interacting together on a daily basis. The strategic marketing director of ALPHA N explains: "The MNC is inevitably going to impart its knowledge, expertise, managerial abilities and best practices when interacting with its host partner".

Other contextual aspects pertaining to informal and trusting relations that grow between partners constitute an undeniable asset in governing the alliance. "Our relation evolved very positively since it is built on trust", confirms the deputy CEO of ALPHA N to which the managing director of ALPHA S adds; "Our partnership was successful because we have a partner that we actually trust".

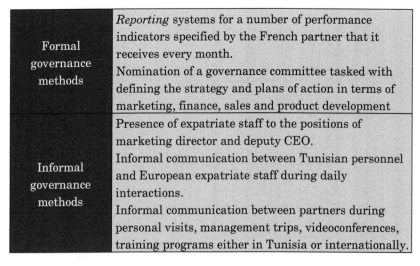

Formal governance methods	*Reporting* systems for a number of performance indicators specified by the French partner that it receives every month. Nomination of a governance committee tasked with defining the strategy and plans of action in terms of marketing, finance, sales and product development
Informal governance methods	Presence of expatriate staff to the positions of marketing director and deputy CEO. Informal communication between Tunisian personnel and European expatriate staff during daily interactions. Informal communication between partners during personal visits, management trips, videoconferences, training programs either in Tunisia or internationally.

Table 4.4. *Governance mechanisms of alliance ALPHA*

The variables of trust and communication justify the atmosphere of cooperation that characterizes the alliance and speed with which they manage conflictive situations. "Coordination is established by all means of communication and information sharing. To govern this alliance, we have put in place all of our standards in order to be in constant communication with the partner and interact constructively, the way video-conferencing allows us to. We have created work-communities that allow file-sharing, opinion exchanges, visiting blogs, etc. We supplied the partner with a professional social network", confirms the IS director of ALPHA N. The deputy CEO of ALPHA N adds: "There is regular communication between us to ensure the governance of the alliance".

4.2. The role of IS in the management of alliance ALPHA

IS represent a central issue and a key factor to the success of all activities within ALPHA N. Toward the end of the 1990s, ALPHA N was using heterogeneous information systems such as ERP, specifically J.D. Edwards, Providence... This presented real integration problems. Data frameworks were different, which led to gaps that proved hard to bridge. Furthermore, each department did not have access to the same information. The information system director at ALPHA N explains: "This confusion of software was neither stable nor reliable for technical reasons". Add to that the total management and support cost of ALPHA N's information systems, due to the fact that the deployed software lacked uniformity harmonization and alignment with the global strategy of the company.

In 2003, the French partner embarked on a project of cross-organization integration based on the deployment of an integrated information system that would use an SAP architecture to optimize and rationalize the computing investments while emphasizing synergies on a global scale.

The French IS director confirms: "Our group launched a standardization of ERP plan 10 years ago, implementing SAP as well as its best business practices. This integration is present in all business units at a global scale, replacing all sorts of ERP, such as Providence, JD Edwards and others, in France and in the world. Our objective is to accompany and accelerate growth through innovation and efficient and effective software solutions". To do this, it developed its IT department to 300 people, armed with considerable integration expertise in order to orchestrate these various systems and technological environments.

Homogenizing the IS for ALPHA N on a world level also improved monitoring within the strategic alliance in terms of activity, operations and use of resources, without necessarily having to wait for reports. ALPHA N's IS director considers that: "We must align our partner's IS with our own. We must ensure that in the long term, we have always configured our IS to automate control". Yet, looking at the case of Tunisian company ALPHA S, this did not happen, despite the efforts of the MNC to convince the Tunisian CEO to consolidate the IS of their joint company. "We will not be able to consolidate the capital of the joint-venture despite our efforts to convince the Tunisian CEO.   Annual meetings with the partner always raise this issue", admits the Tunisian information system and management control director, who goes on to say: "It isn't just about integrating an information system, but rather knowing how to model it. Setting up an SAP system generates yearly costs beyond just initial costs. Certain companies have a business model that simply does not support high software expenses". "There will always be a certain resistance from the partner to adopt our business operating model, which displeases us", adds the IS governance director at ALPHA N.

Before sealing the strategic alliance, ALPHA S did not have an ERP: "We didn't have an integrated IS", confirms the managing director of ALPHA S. The Tunisian company had a number of compatibility and salary management tools, but not that of a system that integrated all of its processes and functions: "We had a few compatibility and salary management tools, but no integrated software solutions like CAPE (Computer-aided production engineering) or CMMS (Computerized mainframe management system) quality processing, purchase management", according to the General Manger of ALPHA S.

The accounting system was totally centralized and made up of heterogeneous, non-integrated, non-interfaced applications. The applications for supplier accounting, supply management and general accounting, while being from the same developer, worked autonomously. Inventory management and production flows were performed by hand, which often led to errors or omissions. Workflow management for sales and marketing were non-integrated. "Before, a manufacturer would perform their own reporting on an Excel spreadsheet and the results they would have there would not always coincide with the results found by the accountants. We also had difficulties commenting on our results and having reliable information", explains the managing director of ALPHA S. This situation led to problems relating to information management, non-optimization of management processes of accounting and cash flows, the absence of integrity or even asymmetry in information processing particularly at an internal level.

The alliance with French company ALPHA N was accompanied by a remodeling from the ground-up of the Tunisian company's IS as well as the digitization of management and operation processes, "in order to better govern the company with powerful computing tools", as stated by the General Manager of ALPHA S. Therefore, the strategic alliance with ALPHA N helped to optimize the management processes of accounting and cash flows and the integrity and symmetry of information because of the introduction of a new sophisticated and efficient IS. The IS governance director of ALPHA N states "the integration of a new IS turned out to be necessary to accelerate, secure and control the business model of this alliance".

At an informational level, the Tunisian company opted for the latest version of the integrated management JD Edwards software package in 2001 to integrate all alliance-related activities on a single database, maintain homogeneous and coherent information flows and minimize incompatibilities resulting from information asymmetry? The database is composed of nine modules that cover supplying (purchases and inventory management of raw materials), supplier accounting, fixed-asset management, production management, maintenance management or even sales management (sales and management of the finished product), client accounting, analytical accounting, and general accounting. The Management control and IS director of ALPHA S tells us: "We integrated the purchases and inventory management modules with the accounting module. Then, the sales function which was integrated with client accounting and general accounting. Supplier accounting which has already been integrated and remained...". However, the payment and treasury modules are managed by specific applications but are interfaced with the general accounting module of the JD Edwards software package. "This project had the advantage of integrating functions, making our accounting plan, reviewing all functions, reviewing cost centers, setting up our partner's accounting plan", confirms the Management Control and IS director of ALPHA S.

Nonetheless, the ERP system integrated within ALPHA S differs to that of its partner ALPHA N despite the efforts produced by the latter to consolidate both IS, due to costs from changing and maintaining governance. The management control and information system director of ALPHA S confirms: "We will continue to use our own information system for reasons of cost and adapting to change".

The integration of IS emphasized regular communications between partners thanks to the use of communication tools such as e-mails and cross-organization video conferencing. "Coordination is established thanks to all means of communication and information sharing", according to the IS director of ALPHA N. And in a joint perspective, the IS governance director of ALPHA N adds: "our partners have connected to our messaging system and our social network". Due to this, the quality of information has considerably improved and costs relating to file transferring have significantly decreased. Times required for information collection, reentry, transfer and explanation of numbers is now used for analysis and interpretations which explains, in part, the relevance of the decisions made by the alliance.

The decisional dimension of this alliance is characterized by relevance and efficiency because of available information. "Our partner can easily access our database and share our information from France. They have open, real time and unencumbered access", confirms the managing director of ALPHA S, who highlights the role of the IS in decision making "The IS is designed to provide reliable information which don't necessarily rely on the accuracy of accountants, managers or financial advisors. The correlation of information results primarily from the IS". This is confirmed by the French interface, which highlights the importance of the IS in making decisions within the alliance. "The IS represents a facilitating tool for decision making within the alliance, due to key charts, reporting, analyses, and performance indicators it reproduces. These elements will allow the partners to redirect the business if necessary and make decisions", according to the IS director of ALPHA N.

The IS generates reliable information and manages the risks of the alliance thanks to the communication of periodic activity reports on a number of indicators such as turnover, production volume, financial statuses, etc. As explained by the management control and information system director at ALPHA S: "at d+4 of every month, we do the reports, even though we are not consolidated. We also do a Semestrial and Annual report". "I believe the IS plays a key role in managing the risks relating to the alliance. We need to make sure that the figures we send out to the group's financial committee are exact and reliable", the IS Governance director of ALPHA N adds. Let us, however, highlight that the activity reports are communicated according to a predefined model from the MNC to circumvent issues with representation, information processing and heterogeneous data. Standardization responds to a need for integration that allows the French partner to reconcile the information, correlate actions and synchronize data.

To conclude, the quality of the information system in broadcasting, sharing and capitalizing knowledge is a tool for development and growth to ALPHA S. The management control and information system director of ALPHA S states the following: "For our alliance to provide added-value, we need our IS to acquire the expertise and KPI[4] provided by our partner".

---

4 KPI: Key Performance Indicators.

5

Case DELTA

5.1. Characteristics of alliance DELTA

5.1.1. *Organizational form of the alliance*

DELTA S, a Tunisian company that deals in dairy products, chose to form an alliance with DELTA N, a daughter company to a French agribusiness group specializing in the production and distribution of milk for general consumption.

This strategic alliance takes the form of a licensing contract, the terms of which are agreed upon by the allies along with the objective of the alliance and the obligations of each party. "It is a licensing agreement created in 2006. Company DELTA N receives royalties on the sales revenue. In return, we use its brand to commercialize our products and receive their technical assistance", states the marketing director of DELTA S.

As per the terms of contract signed by both companies, DELTA S uses the brand and expertise of its partner DELTA N in exchange for royalties paid out on the sales revenue of its line of products.

DELTA S, on the other hand, must conform to its partners' policies and instructions in terms of supply, production and commercialization of the licensed product while using its technical and technological expertise.

It is a licensing agreement created in 2006 between the French company (DELTA N) and the Tunisian company (DELTA S) that states the production and commercialization of dairy products by the Tunisian partner using the French partner's brand name in return for royalty shares of sales revenue.

Partner DELTA S[1]	Partner DELTA N[2]
– Anonymous company created in 1975, operating on the stock exchange since 1993, privatized in 2006	– Subsidiary of France's largest dairy cooperative group. Created in 1971, it has since become the leader on the French market for drinking milk in 2008
– Total staff (2011): 397	– Total staff (2011): 1090 in France
– Turnover (2011): €42.80 million	– Turnover (2011): €1.18 billion
– Activity: the production and commercialization of a large range of dairy production the market: third largest operator in the Tunisian milk industry with an average market share of 15%	– Activity: the production and distribution of drinking
	– Market share: 30 % of the drinking milk market in France
– Strategy: cost control, improving quality, diversifying products and developing in terms of attractive packaging	– Strategy: product differentiation (long-life bottles, cartons with twist-caps, flavored milk, fortified milk, baby milk), creativity, innovation, internationalization

Table 5.1. *Presentation of alliance DELTA*[3]

1 Corresponds to the name we gave the Tunisian company to respect their confidentiality requests.

2 Corresponds to the name we gave the European company to respect their confidentiality requests.

3 The data in Table 4.1 have been collected from institutional websites from two companies that allowed us to get a sense of their activities, their organizations, their missions, etc., beyond the semidirective interviews performed with the two partners of alliance DELTA between October 2012 and June 2013.

5.1.2. Ends sought by each party

DELTA N is part of a French group that has been the market leader in production and distribution of dairy products since 2008. "Our group was created in 1971 and has since become the market-leader in the dairy industry in France, thanks to a number of original initiatives that have marked the history of our products, in particular the tri-layer bottles, flavored milk, fortified milk, baby-milk and the cartons with twist-caps", confirms the marketing director of DELTA N.

In a bid to ensure international geographic expansion, DELTA N elected to develop partnership strategies with agribusiness groups in areas where the dairy industry is in full growth, such as Northern Africa, India, and South-America. "In order to develop, we first pursued an export strategy, of our products over to Europe", confirms the industrial director of DELTA N who then goes on "Then, we set our sights on the rest of the world. Since 1990, we have been developing franchises, licenses and partnerships everywhere in the world".

The strategic alliance with DELTA S represents, for DELTA N, a means for development and a way to penetrate the Tunisian market. "We formed a strategic alliance with DELTA S in the hopes to enter an emerging market such as Tunisia's, develop our brand and our products and build an international network", explains, to that effect, the industrial director of DELTA N. Furthermore, the Tunisian company represents a source of profit allowing DELTA N to minimize their risk and costs relating to the implementation of a new entity while benefitting from a long adaptation period to local consumer behaviors. The marketing director of DELTA N then explains: "the strategic alliance allows us to cut implementation and investment costs". The industrial director of DELTA N continues: "We opted for a licensing contract with DELTA S for financial reasons. We wish to realize industrial performances at minimal costs to remain competitive on the market".

Meanwhile, DELTA S has used the licensing contract option to consolidate its position on the local dairy market and to acquire expertise. "Through this alliance, we are looking to improve our position on the Tunisian market", states the R&D director of DELTA S. The management control director adds: "Our objective consists of benefitting from the technical assistance, training and the technological expertise of our partner in order to improve our brand".

The strategic alliance with a globally powerful partner such as DELTA N allows DELTA S to defend against its own technical deficiencies and the problems with quality and lack of expertise. "We concluded a strategic alliance with DELTA N because we had technical problems surrounding the packaging and quality of the product", confirms DELTA S' R&D director.

On the production level, the host partner aims to acquire new processes and new techniques in order to innovate product concepts and perfect the production process. The marketing director at DELTA S adds: "We have looked to receive training on milk production. Our partner holds real experience in that area".

On the marketing level, the alliance with DELTA N allows DELTA S to introduce both new commercialization techniques and marketing processes to improve their product line and their position on the market. The marketing director at DELTA S states: "We have formed an alliance with DELTA N to benefit from their marketing experience and their experience with successful partnerships in emerging countries". To, this, the management control director adds: "We are hoping to acquire new expertise on the product, advertising, marketing, sales, etc.".

5.1.3. *Resources committed by the partners*

The contributions from DELTA N to this alliance are mainly intangible and vary in nature. DELTA N's image and its brand of products are internationally renowned. "DELTA N is the French market-leader in drinking milk", confirms the marketing director of DELTA N, then going on to say: "We offered our partner the opportunity to use our knowledge and international brand to assist its development on the market". Furthermore, DELTA N has used high-level quality-assessment procedures since 1993 to gain their customers' trust. The Industrial director of DELTA N states, in turn: "All of our production sites are certified according to ISO 9001-V2000 norms".

On a technical level, DELTA N grants access to its technological expertise to help optimize its partner's production process. "We are committed to investing in our partner's production site to support them in their development of new industrial processes, product commercialization, improvement of market positioning... There is ongoing technical assistance organized over a number of times every year", claims DELTA N's marketing director. "Our partner guarantees permanent technical assistance", explains the R&D director of DELTA S.

At a quality control level, DELTA N's resources are characterized by new analysis processes and quality control methods compliant with European standards in order to preserve its product's brand image on an international scale. "The quality control models, the analysis and manufacturing protocols were perfected following our alliance with DELTA N", explains DELTA S' R&D director, who goes on to say: "We adapted the quality control and analysis methods from DELTA N".

From a marketing perspective, the contributions from DELTA N correspond to the requirements of new programs and marketing campaigns and new operation methods of distributing the finished subcontracted product. "Our partner allows us to use their marketing knowledge. They share new knowledge with us about which marketing strategies to use, product launch policies, etc.", according to the marketing director of DELTA S.

On a relational level, the French partner assists DELTA S in selecting suppliers of raw materials and packaging. "Our partner can help in selecting the best packaging suppliers", confirms the Marketing director of DELTA S and continues: "When we decided to launch a new product on the market, we consulted with our partner to ask them to help us in choosing manufacturing machines and the best suppliers. DELTA N belongs to an international group with an interesting portfolio of suppliers".

Furthermore, the elements made available by DELTA S are essentially tangible in nature, including infrastructure, technologies, equipment. "Our resources include the supply chain, dairy products and distribution methods", DELTA S' management control director explains. Aside from tangible resources, the Tunisian company offers its partner the opportunity to enter a new potential market. DELTA N's industrial director states: "Our partner allows us to develop and acquire large market shares in Tunisia".

From a quality perspective, the Tunisian company put in place an environmental management system compliant with international norms. To this effect, the R&D director at DELTA S states: "Our company was certified ISO 9001 and ISO 14000. We have implemented the integrated management system. We are doing everything to obtain ISO 22000 certification".

As for human resources, the Tunisian company has committed, since the beginning of the strategic alliance with DELTA N, to developing human resources, on the one hand,

and the improvement of its standard, on the other hand, by reinforcing their management level, for instance. DELTA S' management control director confirms: "Our staff are qualified. Spending on training is constantly increasing in order to improve our personnel's abilities". As for sales, the Tunisian company has emphasized its commitment to boosting commercial activity through the creation of a transport network for collecting and distributing drinking milk on the Tunisian market. "Our company has acquired inventory and logistics means in a bid to ensure better sales performance", confirms the management control director.

Commitments	
Tunisian company DELTA S	European company DELTA N
– Strong position on a potential market – Large financial capacity – A large local distribution network	– Global leader – Key abilities and knowledge in R&D, manufacturing methods and processes, marketing – A sterling brand name and reputation – A competitive relational network

Table 5.2. *The contributions of both partners of alliance DELTA*

5.1.4. *Perimeter of activity of the alliance*

This strategic alliance is characterized by strong integration of the partners in the value chain covering R&D activities, supply, manufacturing, marketing and distribution. According to the marketing director at DELTA S "Our partner attempts to support us on a technical level. They play a determining role in marketing and production assistance".

At the technical level, the MNC assists its counterpart in order to acquire manufacturing techniques and processes required to produce its licensed product. "Our partner informs us on innovating formulations and processes such as flavored milk, fortified milk, etc. Our partner provides its crucial technological knowledge to ensure our development", explains DELTA S' marketing director. This generates experience and develops our line of products that benefits DELTA S. The Tunisian R&D director then states: "We have diversified our range of products with variations like flavored milk, fortified milk, baby milk, following our alliance with the French partner".

From an R&D perspective, the Tunisian company obtains the control of innovative processes. "When we launched the tri-layer bottle, we called upon our partner multiple times, because this type of packaging requires new expertise which we did not have", confirms DELTA S' R&D director before stating "The control models, analysis protocols, manufacturing protocols, all the way to the release of the product were perfected following our alliance with DELTA N".

On a marketing level, the marketing director of DELTA S explains: "there are lots of exchanges of new marketing knowledge, though they are limited to the licensed product".

1	Production
2	Quality control
3	Commercialization

Table 5.3. *Perimeter of the alliance*

5.1.5. *Governance model of the alliance*

The assistance provided by the French partner involves respecting a number of previously mentioned instructions from the licensing contract, which cover practically every area.

On a production level, the supply of raw materials, product packaging and conditioning is managed by the French partner in a centralized fashion so as to maintain the quality of their products. DELTA N's industrial director states: "The quality of the milk is a weak-point for DELTA S and a major impediment to their development. It suffers from insufficient nutritional value from a physical, chemical and biological stand-point, which represents an important risk factor. For this reason, we insist that they source their milk from our suppliers". The R&D director adds to this point: "When we wanted to enter the local market with bottled sterilized milk, it was with the transparent bottle under the Elben[4] brand. However, our partner was using the tri-layer bottle as it preserved the quality of the milk slightly better. We opted to use the tri-layer bottle to debut the brand with our partner. Importing this packaging was done along with our partner. We are the only supplier of bottled conditioned milk on the Tunisian market since 2006".

From a marketing perspective, the host partner must comply with the MNC's marketing strategy and plans. The marketing director of DELTA S states the following: "During our meetings, we present our marketing action plans, relating to the type of packaging for example, or the type of communication. The difficulty is validating any sub-lines, because everyone can't have the same vision. And when that's the case, we are not a majority voice in the marketing decisions. Our partner has final say". Information flow exchanges, i.e. the marketing directors for DELTA S and DELTA N, are continuous thanks to the use of communication tools to pursue and share improvements necessary for the product, the recipe, the packaging, the launch and the communication policy. "We are collecting information that we then share with DELTA N regarding

---

4 Commercial name of the Tunisian product.

market data and competition", confirms the DELTA S marketing director.

On a commercial level, DELTA N has implemented commercialization process monitoring measures for the licensed product. "As we are using our partner's commercial brand to sell our products, we have to comply with their commercial techniques. In fact, we are equipped with new logistic and storage means to ensure better sales performance", confirms the marketing director of DELTA S.

It is apparent that the strategic decisions made within this relationship are centralized around DELTA N. The marketing director of DELTA S states: "DELTA N gives us work directives surrounding production, marketing and the strategy we should use. Our partner makes sure its brand is not damaged in any way by ensuring we comply with any particularly action or strategy". "The plans of action set by the partner must be executed to the letter", says the R&D director of DELTA S.

Thus, the local company has no room for maneuverability and follows and applies instructions from DELTA N in compliance with their contract specifications. "Strategic decision-making always concerns the partner that has control and validation power. This means that we submit our plans of action and the partner validates it", states the marketing director of DELTA S. The marketing director for DELTA N adds to this: "We entrust our partner with a brand that they will use while respecting the quality of the product and the customers' expectations".

As for matters of objective realization, the French partner has implemented a monthly reporting system. The activity reports that are communicated only concern the industrial and commercial fields. The financial status and the internal and external audit reports do not get transferred to the MNC. "Neither internal or external audit reports, nor reports to the auditor are sent to the partner. Profitably data is also not sent to them", specifies the management control director of DELTA S.

This means that control is performed via regular visits by the director for Northern Africa and the marketing director of the French company on-site at DELTA S. "There are also regular partnership meetings in order to observe the goings-on from up-close", states DELTA N's industrial director, adding: "We perform meetings even when things are going well. Preventive meetings are pretty frequent".

The French partner can also perform audit missions surrounding DELTA S' production, quality and sales functions, to maintain their product's quality and its international brand image "We perform audits to ensure the product's manufacturing standards and its quality", confirms the marketing director of DELTA N.

Other than formal mechanisms, the MNC provides training and demonstrations for the staff at DELTA S. This training can take place on-site at DELTA S or in France. "As it's an international partnership and to confront cultural and linguistic hurdles, it is worth being close to the partner to organize training sessions", the industrial director at DELTA N confirms. The marketing director then adds: "In this relationship, there is strong support from our training staff who will perform training sessions for the personnel at DELTA S on industrial, themes, marketing and sales", then: "Our training staff are experts in the fields of R&D, industry, commerce and marketing. DELTA S personnel can also receive training at our facilities in France".

This way, training offers possibilities for staff at DELTA S to internalize the best production methods and acquire new expertise and skills. "We have made training programs for manufacturing staff and R&D teams. As a head of laboratory, I followed a training program in conception and innovative product development", the DELTA S R&D director confirms. "I undertake regular trainings to improve my abilities", explains the Tunisian marketing director.

Furthermore, human resources at DELTA S can attend conventions and international shows. "This year for example, I will be in Paris at the end of October to attend the SIAL, which is an exchange forum designed to discover the newest culinary trends and innovations that will shape tomorrow's markets. Our partner keeps us informed of conventions and international forums", the R&D director of DELTA S confirms.

Formal governance mechanisms	Implementation of a governance committee tasked with defining the strategy and plans of action for production, marketing and sales and controlling their deployment.
	Implementation of a reporting system surrounding quantities produced and sales figures for the licensed product
	Annual audit
	The business ethics chart and code of conduct
Informal governance mechanisms	Informal communication between partners during personal visits, meetings, management trips and videoconferences
	Training programs on-site at the Tunisian partner's company

Table 5.4. *Governance mechanisms of alliance DELTA*

5.2. Role of IS in managing alliance DELTA

IS is a key factor for company DELTA N, having accompanied it throughout its internationalization procedure. DELTA N is equipped with integrated software packages that manage a variety of functional applications, sophisticated and modern means of communication, tools for managing customer relations and the logistics chain and decision support software. "Our group uses dedicated applications such as GENERIX (billing), MFGPRO (manufacturing support), LOGYS (inventory management), and CODA (accounting)", according to the logistics director at DELTA N.

In accounting and finance, a number of archiving and invoice digitization solutions have been implemented. DELTA N has also introduced a financial consolidation software suite and a treasury management application. In logistics and sales management, the logistics director at DELTA N confirms: "The LOGISTICS MANAGER SUITE has been operational since 2010. It has been implemented on our production sites and our logistics platforms in order to unify all of our logistic governance processes". In the human resources department, DELTA N is fitted with an account payable tool salary payments and previsions management software for upcoming skill and employment requirements.

DELTA N has also begun implementing an integrated management software on all manufacturing sites to support all types of inventory management. "Logys is a solution we have implemented to ensure logistic execution and traceability on all of our sites. Interfaces with our ERP system are now stable", explains the Supply Chain Information Systems of group DELTA N[5].

DELTA N's information system thus endures the crucial informational integration necessary to its projects. The industrial director there explains: "Our IS is the source of indicators that we use to direct projects for the company. To do so, it must converge with the objective of the governance committee, tasked with directing the project".

---

5 This information is published on the website of DELTA N.

Furthermore, the information system at DELTA S allows the integration of a number of applications for accounting, sales, purchases, client and supplier invoicing... "We installed an ERP in 2008. Before then, we used another software package that did not encompass all of these functions. This led to numerous issues such as confidential information being leaked, errors, lack of control and time wasting. We considered the use of an ERP and organized training sessions for our staff", explains the management control director of DELTA S.

On an interorganizational level, the strategic partners trade e-mails and participate in phone conferences to navigate their joint business functions. "The digital communication systems that we share are useful to the success of this partnership, considering the geographic distance", states DELTA N's marketing director. To which the management control director at DELTA S adds: "There are information exchanges among partners using classic methods such as e-mail, telephone and physical meetings".

Let us, however, specify that the French partner has secured the access to its information system in a way that its strategic databases are confidential and its partner cannot access them. "We have not implemented a joint portal because the access risk of information is managed and limited. It's confidential", insists DELTA S marketing director. Information, whatever its nature, is obtained on demand from the Tunisian partners. "If I am to perform a marketing action in a particular area, I must first know the performance information of that area. This is cross-referenced with sales information sent to the partner to justify my request", the DELTA S marketing director explains.

Reporting is implemented following a pre-established model specified by DELTA N based on a number of indicators to avoid issues stemming from the representation and interpretation of heterogeneous information. The industrial director for DELTA N states: "The IS is our main source of indicators that will inform the governance committee and affect their decisions. For this, it must correspond to the committee's objectives. It is important that the governance committee have all necessary information at their disposal so that they are capable of precise analyses and able to make pertinent decisions". "Any information sent under a different format will cause usage and tracking difficulties. Reports must use a specific format to assist result explanations, and how they are calculated. If we are not clear in explaining what we expect, there will always be a gap between what we are aiming for and what we receive", DELTA N's industrial director confirms, adding: "It is very important to use a specification sheet to precisely note our expectations of each partner. The IS must subsequently meet our expectations".

Thus, the standardization of information representation corresponds to the French partner's need to conciliate information, correlate actions and synchronize data. The French marketing director explains: "We try to make sure our standards are respected by the partner".

DELTA S has, therefore, established a reporting system that allows them to isolate different applications, dashboards and decision-making statistics for different fields. On an industrial level, the host partner compiles a monthly activity report that contains information pertaining to manufacturing quantities, yield rates, number of customer claims. "We have to prepare a monthly report for the partner on the quantities produced and a statement of any claims or defects. We can also prepare a specific report upon request from our partner during a visit or for any other specific reason", the DELTA S R&D director reports. On a commercial and marketing level, the host partner must transmit an activity report including all information inherent to communication and marketing expenses, consumer panels, redemption rates following a marketing campaign, etc. "We inform the partner on the volume and quantity of products sold by geographic area, as well as the variation in that amount on a month-by-month basis or in comparison to the evolution of another marketing campaign. The management control team here at DELTA S establishes the information requested by the partner", explains the Tunisian management control director.

Case KAPPA

6.1. Characteristics of alliance KAPPA

This is a sublicensing contract which formed between Tunisian company KAPPA S and French company KAPPA N in 2010 concerns the manufacturing and assembly of automotive connectors.

Partner KAPPA S[1]	Partner KAPPA N[2]
– Anonymous company created in 1992 – Market leader in electrical wires and cables for use in the automotive industry – First partner of the 10 major producers of automotive wiring harnesses, and of major automotive manufacturers – Staff (2011): 800 – Turnover (2011): €550 million – Strategy: provide partners with high-quality products, optimized logistics and innovative services offering technological solutions and cost reduction solutions	– Anonymous company created in 2003 – Designer, manufacturer and supplier of electronic and electronic systems for use in the automotive industry – Staff (2011): 1200 – Turnover (2011): €1.25 billion – Geographic settlement: 30 sites throughout the world including five factories in France

Table 6.1. *Presentation of alliance KAPPA*[3]

1 Corresponds to the name we gave the Tunisian company to respect their confidentiality requests.
2 Corresponds to the name we gave the European company to respect their confidentiality requests.

6.1.1. *Organizational form of the alliance*

The relation between the Tunisian company and the French group began in 2010 under the form of a sub-contracting license for the manufacturing and assembly of automotive connectors. "In March 2010, an agreement was concluded between the two Directors. This partnership regarded the manufacturing of electrical automotive wiring", confirms the Tunisian Finance and Administration director.

6.1.2. *Ends sought by both partners*

Company KAPPA N signed a subcontracting agreement with the Tunisian company in order to develop in the Northern African market with better quality products at lower costs. "With a low presence in Northern Africa, it was important for us to penetrate this market in a way that emphasized our development", states the foreign IS director. "Our partner targeted Tunisia to increase its market-shares and internationalize itself", adds the Tunisian Finance and Administration director, thus highlighting the European party's motivations. The potential deciding factors of this strategic move consist, for the French partner, of reducing uncertainty by sharing the costs and risks that come with this type of *"greenfields"*[4] expansion onto the Tunisian market, in particular during the period of instability following the Tunisian revolution. "Due to the revolution, the partner did not have the possibility to enter Tunisia directly because the political climate was very unstable. Their objective was to ally with a Tunisian company in order to

3 The data presented in Table 6.1 have been collected from the institutional websites of both companies which allowed us to get a sense of their activities, their organizations, their missions, etc., beyond the semidirective interviews performed with the two partners of alliance KAPPA.

4 Direct creation of an autonomous subsidiary or unit.

enter the Northern African market", comments the Tunisian Finance and Administration director. The French IS director supports this, stating: "To reduce the risks of failure, we preferred to create an alliance rather than going in alone. It was an excellent opportunity to ally ourselves with KAPPA S in the context of an expansion into Northern Africa".

The Tunisian company used this opportunity to consolidate its assets and benefit from the European partner's experience in the overseas automotive industry. The Tunisian IS director expresses the following: "The alliance was created to allow us to acquire skills and knowledge from the partner, who has demonstrated technological ability in the field of automotive connections".

The primary motivation for the Tunisian company consists of mastering the "plastic injection" technique as well as acquiring knowledge and abilities necessary to improve their position on the international market with high-quality products at reduced costs. The Tunisian Financial Administrative director explains: "Our main objective that justifies this partnership is the acquisition of a new skill: injection. While being accepted in the assembly industry, we still needed to master this technique. We therefore made sure that the contract included the transfer of knowledge relating to injection".

6.1.3. *Resources committed by the partners*

The French partner ranks among the top global manufacturers in the field of connectivity. It develops and supplies innovative and high-grade products for a wide range of industrial and commercial applications. "Our partner counts among the top global manufacturers in the field of connectivity. They develop and supply their clients with innovative and high quality products. Their activity consists of parts assembly, injection and commercialization", the Tunisian director of Finance and Administration.

Therefore, the French company operates on a large number of innovative projects assembly and injection of automotive parts and components, which rely on their technical expertise and experience. This option gives the host partner considerable benefits in terms of knowledge and new technologies. "The object of this alliance consists of parts assembly, injection and commercialization. Injection represents a new skill provided by the partner in order to improve our development", states the Tunisian director of Finance and Administration.

Beyond the knowledge they share with their MNC, the latter also offers ongoing technical assistance to the local company helping them improve their productivity. "Our partner often advises us on how to improve yields and productivity", the Tunisian director of Finance and Administration confirms, adding: "The alliance has considerably improved our performance in assembly, while minimizing costs through their experience".

The strategic alliance therefore represents a source of knowledge for the host partner. The MNC's experience includes best practices, which contributes to updating the local company's personnel's skills and consolidating its technical and technological assets. Through this alliance, the host partner has benefitted from the MNC's market experience of wiring and harnesses in the automotive industry. "This partnership has allowed us to improve our performance and become more competent in terms of assembly, also minimizing our costs through the effect of experience. Production time has therefore gradually decreased", the Tunisian Financial and Administrative director confirms. Furthermore, the latter company will demonstrate its acquisition and use of its strategic partner's assets because of its absorptive ability as well as its strategic intention of acquiring a perfect mastery of "plastic injection".

The Tunisian company has committed tangible resources which included facilities, equipment and personnel resources. KAPPA S provides its partner with a production site equipped with high-quality materials and technologies allowing them to develop the project to their expected standards. "KAPPA S provides the premises, the workforce, the equipment, purchases the raw materials and the components that allow the alliance to function", explains the Tunisian Facilities director.

From a human resources perspective, the technicians, engineers and executives working at the Tunisian company are competent and highly qualified. The Tunisian Facilities director comments: "The partnership agreement includes the provision of the workforce required for production".

Aside from tangible resources, the Tunisian partner is a local market leader in electrical wiring for use in the automotive industry and boasts one of the highest considered brand images, which represents an asset to value creation. "The notoriety and brand image of our company play a deciding role in automotive projects. We are widely recognized on the market for our proficiency in assembly and wiring", states the Tunisian Finance and Administration director, to which the general manager adds: "In the field of automotive wiring, we sit among the largest partners of manufacturers such as Mercedes, Volkswagen, PSA, Renault, Fiat, BMW, Opel, Ford, etc.".

Commitments	
Tunisian company KAPPA S	European company KAPPA N
– Access to an equipped manufacturing facility – Access to qualified staff	– Global leader – Crucial abilities and expertise in the area of manufacturing and quality control processes and methods – High-level brand name and reputation

Table 6.2. *Commitments of both partners of alliance KAPPA*

Quality is fundamental and crucial for the host partner, who has always valued the merit of excellence, constantly offering innovative and high-quality solutions on both local and foreign markets. The Tunisian general manager explains: "Our clients' perception of the quality of our performance is testimony to the reliability of our quality policies. This has been achieved by a shared culture that values quality throughout our organization and the implementation of efficient and effective quality control management systems in compliance with standards ISO/TS 16949 and ISO 14001".

6.1.4. *Perimeter of activity of alliance KAPPA*

The roles and missions of each partner are mentioned in the contract. "Our relation is defined by a contract that clearly outlines each party's roles and responsibilities. Everything is specified and established according to our respective capacities and funds. We are bound on either side to respect the clauses of the contract", states, to this effect, the Tunisian Facilities director.

The contract states that the host partner is expected to source their raw materials and components from the partner, recruit staff and comply with deadlines and recommendations specified by the latter. "The partner has trained the personnel in compliance with the requirements set by our company's leadership. The entire manufacturing, logistics, purchases and quality management team are involved in this alliance", confirms the French company's IS director.

In return, the French partner supplies its partner with all the details and different steps concerning the products' manufacturing, supervise its progress and provide technical assistance. "The partner's involvement depends on the progression of the project", the Tunisian Facilities director comments, "In our alliance, we distinguish between two levels of involvement for the personnel: one tasked with recruitment and training, manufacturing and quality control which involve us. A second, tasked with technical assistance, IS implementation and knowledge transfer which involves the partner company".

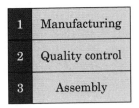

1	Manufacturing
2	Quality control
3	Assembly

Table 6.3. *Alliance perimeter*

6.1.5. *Governance model of the alliance*

The governance process of the alliance is characterized by the joint involvement of the partners in order to ensure the activities are carried out smoothly. From the host partner's side, "involvement concerns the financial aspect, quality, engineering and workforce. It is considerable and applies to all operational, functional and strategic levels", the Tunisian Facilities director comments. The MNC, on the other hand, calls upon a site manager who ensures the progress of work on schedule and the execution of plans of action and objectives in compliance with the specification sheet. "The partner has nominated a site manager to minimize claims and maintain the quality of its products", confirms the local Financial Administrative director.

Nonetheless, the MNC's involvement in the governance of the alliance is prorated over the progression of the project. "Our partner's involvement depends of the degree of progression of the project. During the creation phase, the legal and financial directors were the ones involved in the elaboration of the project. During the production stage, the production and quality agents take-over, hence, the partner's involvement evolves proportionally with the progression of the design", comments the Tunisian Facilities director.

The coordination of activities in the alliance is based on the cooperation between the two managers of each of the sites who jointly define all action plans and production schedules that must be met. "We establish a specifications sheet that outlines each step that needs to be respected. The managers of both sites participate in regular phone conferences in order to verify their check-list together. If modifications are needed, dialogues between both partners is imperative", comments the Tunisian Facilities director. "We are obligated to comply to a production schedule that has been previously agreed upon with the partner according to our factory's capabilities and resources", adds the Tunisian IS Director. Nonetheless, during the execution of plans of action, the host partner must apply the interface instructions to the letter. In this vein, the Tunisian director of Finance and Administration states: "We must respect all outlined details for the manufacturing of joint products, this includes the model, the format, the part designation, the reference, the quantity etc."

For the management of day-to-day activities, a team was formed of a foreign site manager and a number of other operators by the European partner in order to supervise the different processes of the project, reduce communication problems and limit delays and surcharges linked to eventual productivity flaws in the Tunisian team. The Tunisian company's Financial Administrative director comments: "Our partner nominated a Facilities director, a quality control team formed by a head of the department of quality, an engineer, a logistics manager and a financial manager".

As for the achievement of strategic objectives and action plans, the partners have cross-examined project reviews, frequent meetings and reporting.

Project reviews and meetings are organized to optimize the use of production results and the solutions to problems encountered. "During meetings, each of the partners establishes an activity report authorizing necessary comparisons and adjustments during group decisions", the Tunisian Financial Administrative director explains. "Regular follow-up meetings take place once a week during which both teams meet up and analyze the production results, assess partner realizations, define possible gaps and how to solve them", the French IS director confirms, "What's more, more formal meetings respond to project reviews where the results are displayed along with any problems, plans of action for monitoring activity, etc. Furthermore, there is a higher level of monitoring which takes the form of CEO meetings between the French and Tunisian CEOs".

Control is therefore performed through frequent and regular audits. The MNC did, in fact, perform an audit targeting the existence of environmental passiveness, dangerous surroundings or natural risks, as soon as the agreement was signed. "The quality control service is regularly audited, once every six months, to establish a diagnostic of any problems such as, for example the increase in faulty wires", explains the Tunisian IS director.

Trust and informal communication remain important dimensions in this relationship that favors the achievement of objectives via satisfying results for both parties. "Our relationship is based on trust. We work in close collaboration", highlights the Tunisian Facilities director, while the French IS director adds: "We have a decentralized structure that responds to our teamwork objectives. The executives and engineers of each team regularly exchange information and knowledge. Permanent and direct contact between partners is crucial in building a strong relationship. We work in teams to guarantee the success of the project. Our objective is the smooth operation of manufacturing combined with product improvement", the French IS director states.

Trips between Europe and Tunisia are frequent in order to ensure that skills and production processes are properly mastered. The MNC frequently organizes training to keep the Tunisian staff up to date. "These training sessions are mainly for the executive staff, in particular the quality manager and the production manager who regularly travel to the French partner's location in France, Romania or even Hungary to improve their skills and knowledge", says the Financial Administrative director. The Tunisian Facilities director continues: "In the early days of our alliance, a team of technicians traveled to France for 2 weeks in order to acquire the best practices from the partner and transmit them to us".

Finally, the partner's presence on site at KAPPA S is a catalyst for the acquisition of new knowledge and updating plans.

Formal governance mechanisms	Standardization of work processes (complying with the European partner's instructions)
	Organizing project reviews in order to establish the specification sheets and follow up on plans of action
	Regular audits
	Presence of foreign personnel such as the site manager
	Digitizing exchanges through the use of an EDI and the use of an electronic messaging system
Informal governance mechanisms	Informal communication via direct contact between the Tunisian and foreign personnel
	Visits, training performed on-site at the Tunisian partner's facilities

Table 6.4. *Governance mechanisms of alliance KAPPA*

Daily interactions allow partnership members to collect information and share knowledge, respond to unpredictable fluctuations, avoid storing obsolete products and improve flexibility. "We take advantage of our partner's knowledge in the sense that we share a common ground. The partner team has played the role of technical assistance especially during the early stages of the collaboration", says the Tunisian Financial Administrative director. "There is daily communication on the ground. I see my counterpart every day since we are located in the same facility. This allows us to exchange thoughts about the progress of the project and any other subject", adds the Tunisian Facilities director.

6.2. The role of IS in managing alliance KAPPA

The French partner decides to adopt a lighter structure, focus on activities closer to its base abilities such as innovation, R&D and marketing and entrust the Tunisian partner with the rest of the activities. These two companies have since increased their number of interactions considerably as well as their exchanges of information.

KAPPA N is equipped with an SAP-type ERP ensuring the defragmentation of functions and the automation of management processes of information and data in real time. The Tunisian company is also equipped with an ERP information system. The benefits of this system are the reduced costs of use and improved efficiency, the acquisition of reliable and precise information in real-time and the optimization of decision-making processes through precise measures and pertinent analyses. The implementation of an ERP is less of a choice and more an obligation in the automotive industry due to the complexity and diversity of the projects, as confirms KAPPA S IS director: "Unlike in some other sectors, an ERP is in no way an option in the automotive industry. In our group, the ERP INFOR LN is the key stone to our entire information system. It boasts a number of completely integrated modules. Our partner asked us before entering the alliance what ERP we used and its level of integration".

On a cross-organizational level, the French partner has implemented an EDI solution that manages the interfacing between the Tunisian partner's database and the applications of its IS. By opting for this solution, the French partner improves the coherence of the information and the automated processing of its productive requirements in order to react quickly to market demands. "We defined how the two systems would interface, automatically communicating information without the need for human intervention. An interface model between two ERP was therefore created. This allows us to transmit our production needs to our partner via our ERP. Information travels automatically through the partner's IS", the French IS director explains. "Information relating to the number of required parts must first be integrated into our IS. It then passes through the interfacing system to the partner's IS who receive the same request. The system then calculates the requirements in raw materials, components, resources and checks the status of available stock in order to send the order". The use of an EDI encourages coordination and cooperation of activities because of reliable information being communicated efficiently. The Tunisian IS director explains: "The use of an EDI improves coordination because it ensures standards of communication between applications as well as interoperability that eliminates incompatibilities between two heterogeneous IS".

The latter therefore confirms that the use of an EDI solution ensures the exchange of digital information using a standardized language with the partner. Therefore, the EDI allows them to circumvent the inefficiency of manual systems and reduce human intervention in the processing of information. "Among the governance committee's missions was the implementation of an EDI interface between both IS", the Tunisian Facilities director confirms. "No matter the IS, there exist interfaces that translate the information from one system to another. The EDI protocols manage all of those transactions".

Furthermore, KAPPA N handles the implementation of an intranet system with the objective of optimizing the communication and sharing of documents and files. "The second type of information pertaining to claims, waste code is obtained via an electronic messaging system", the French IS director explains in turn. Information sharing contributes to reinforcing team spirit, cohesion and an atmosphere of trust between both partners. Nonetheless, KAPPA N protects access. "There is a notion of data confidentiality that we must respect. We cannot just share all the information contained in the partner's IS", the French IS director explains.

For a more efficient coordination of the activities in that alliance, the Tunisian company digitizes information concerning all of its management procedures and functions with the implementation of an EDI, which will ensure the interface between IS applications. "When the partner emits a delivery order at the end of the manufacturing process, the information integrated into its IS is automatically transferred to our IS. When the merchandize is recovered, we validate the information on our system. This way, the IS enables reporting and invoice confirmation for our partner", explains the French IS director.

Reporting enables the analysis of technical indicators and allows the MNC to monitor their action plans and strategic objectives. "Our partner wishes to know the implementation details and diagrams to follow the progress of the project in real time. This approach is accompanied with the translation of all this information as well as its configuration and integration into the information system in order to respond to our partner's requests", the Tunisian IS director explains, to which the Facilities director adds: "We must integrate different types of indicators like production volume, staff, etc. There are dashboards before every department and service, objectives to be met and established plans of actions to meet said objectives, etc.".

7

Case IOTA

7.1. Characteristics of alliance IOTA

7.1.1. *Organizational form of the alliance*

The relationship between the Tunisian firm and the French corporation goes back to 1999 with the development of an offshore platform in Tunisia specialized in the field of engine drive in the automotive industry. Engine drive activity relies on complex design, development, manufacturing, control and integration processes. In the early stages, the relationship between IOTA S and IOTA N only included the design processes while the other aspects that involved precise skills and technologies could only be achieved by an external service provider and were performed by the French partner. As the Tunisian Technical director states: "the offshore contract only involved the software development aspects. The idea is to develop onboard programs to calculate engine drive". In 2002, the Tunisian company developed its own entity and subsequently became legally independent. That same year, it signed a contracting agreement with French partner IOTA N that authorized it to become a veritable strategic partner systematically involved in the design and quality control phases of software for vehicle engine drive. "We are much more involved in the partner's activity. Today, we not only participate in the design stage, but are also involved with development and quality control", the Tunisian Activities director explains, adding: "Between 2003, when I began and today, the number of people working on the partner's projects has multiplied".

It is a licensing contract signed in 2002 between Tunisian company IOTA S and the French corporation IOTA N in the automotive sector.	
Partner IOTA S[1]	*Partner IOTA N*[3]
– Anonymous company created in 1994	– Anonymous company created in 1980
– Staff (2011): 550	– Staff (2011): 1073 in France
– Turnover: € 15.42 million	– Turnover (2011): €11.8 billion
– Geographic presence : four sites in Tunisia and a site in France	– Geographic presence: presence in North America, Asia, Northern Africa and Eastern Europe
– Sector of activity: design and development of software products for the automotive industry; electronics and microelectronics design; engineering of mechanical products: computer assisted design and mechanical simulation, computer assister manufacturing and industrialization process	– Sector of activity: Design, manufacturing and sales of integrated systems and components for the automotive industry
– In 2005: CMMI[2] (level 5) certification	– Strategy: Innovation and sustainable development

Table 7.1. *Presentation of alliance IOTA*[4]

1 Corresponds to the name we gave the Tunisian company to respect their confidentiality requests.

2 CMMI: "Capability Maturity Model & Integration" is a model composed of best practices designed to improve the activities of engineering companies.

3 Corresponds to the name we gave the European company to respect their confidentiality requests.

4 The data in this table have been collected from institutional websites from both companies that allowed us to get a sense of their activities, their organizations, their missions, etc., beyond the semidirective interviews performed with the two partners of alliance IOTA between January 2013 and May 2013.

7.1.2. *Ends sought by each party*

The French corporation IOTA N signed a subcontracting agreement with Tunisian company IOTA S in order to improve their position in the international automotive industry with higher quality products at lower costs. Acquisition of new production and design technologies, reduced R&D costs and the availability of personnel with key skills represent motivations for IOTA N to form an alliance with IOTA S. "The motivations for this alliance are varied. The costs are lower, while the product remains the same, especially since the partner has taken the initiative of performing a quality audit and received a level 5 certification", the French project coordinator explains. Located on a market characterized by its geographic proximity and a strong use of the French language, IOTA N benefits from this conjunction of a high-quality service at a low cost. "Our geographic proximity to France has, no doubt, factored into the decision to create this alliance", confirms the Tunisian project leader, while the French project coordinator states: "The Tunisian partner has the advantage of speaking French in comparison with other partners. This aspect is important, as all specifications are sent in French. Remote meetings also take place in this language".

The Tunisian company used this opportunity of an alliance with French company IOTA N to acquire new skills and consolidate its assets. "We signed an alliance contract with the market-leader in automotive equipment in order to update our company and skills", the Tunisian project leader confirms, to which the software coordinator adds: "Through this alliance, we seek to acquire new knowledge and skills to become independent on all phases of the project and launch our own product".

Thus, the main motivation for the Tunisian company is the mastery of all aspects of the project with the aim of launching their own product comparable to its partner and improving its position on the international market. "We want to become independent and autonomous, to no longer be subcontractors for our partner. Our objective is to grow in size and renown", states the Tunisian software coordinator. "The objective we seek through this partnership is to improve our expertise and emphasize our R&D functions, and develop our innovation ability in order to achieve a better position on an international scale", adds, in turn, the Tunisian technical director.

7.1.3. Resources committed by the partners

The resources at IOTA N's disposal are intangible in nature. They are based on techniques and skills in the field of design. "Thanks to the partner, we have improved our software skills. This makes us more competent in this department", confirms the Tunisian technical director.

IOTA N is a French corporation that specializes in designing, developing and manufacturing automotive equipment. It is involved in innovative and complex projects, allowing the local interface to experience the latest technologies and develop its skills and technical expertise. "In this partnership, our objective is win-win. The host partner benefits from our expertise", states the French Project coordinator. "Our partner provides us with assistance when we encounter difficulties".

The MNC engages in important investments in an attempt to improve the personnel of local human resources. Furthermore, it contributes to developing new positions within the local company. "The projects are implemented by Tunisian engineers through a national contest. The MNC deals with assisting and training these engineers in the required areas", explains the Tunisian Activities director.

With regards to development, the French partner boasts a strong presence throughout Europe, North-America, and in developing countries in Asia, Northern Africa and Eastern Europe, which allows the host partner to consolidate its offer and compete with global operators. "We are present in 29 countries, have 124 production sites, 20 research centers, 36 development centers and 12 distribution platforms", explains the French project coordinator. "Thanks to this collaboration, we have improved our position on an international scale, emphasized our R&D function and ability for technological innovation", the Tunisian technical director explains.

Also, the French partner's experience and good practices allows the Tunisian company to update its personnel skills and consolidate its technical and technological assets. "Thanks to our partner, we have acquired further software skills and are more competent", the Tunisian software coordinator states. The host partner has been able to acquire and capitalize its partner's assets via its absorptive capacity and its strategic intention to launch its own product. "Our personnel resources have been affected for various projects. This has allowed them to undertake various training at different stages of the project", the Tunisian Activities director tells us.

The Tunisian company contributes by providing fundamentally tangible resources such as the facilities, equipment and human resources. The external interface benefits from a production site fitted with equipment and high-end technologies that enables them to develop the project in compliance with its expectations. "We have a platform equipped with highly qualified technical and technological resources at our partner's disposal", the Tunisian Activities director confirms. On a human resources level, the host partner's executive staff and engineers are highly qualified. "Our engineers hold diplomas from the *grandes écoles* and are highly skilled. Our business model is called Men & Materials. We guarantee satisfactory results and excellent quality of service. This is in line with our commitments to the results", states the Tunisian Activities director.

Other than tangible resources, IOTA S is a local market leader in engineering and developing onboard software in the automotive industry, and boasts a considerable brand image and an optimal level of certification, which represents an asset for value creation. "Our company is a market-leader in Tunisia in the engineering sector", explains the Tunisian technical director, who goes on to say: "Quality is our greatest provision. We have submitted to an audit called CMMI and received the highest level of certification. Thanks to this grade, a number of projects are managed in conjunction with our partner, who calls upon us regularly to perform diagnostics and analysis". The host partner is considered an R&D platform for the external interface that elaborates and values our research and development in the field of engineering and new technologies. "Our partner is very satisfied with our relationship, the quality of our services and with the costs, which are lower than those of internalizing this activity", the Tunisian software coordinator tells us.

Commitments	
Tunisian company IOTA S	European company IOTA N
– Qualified personnel – Use of an equipped manufacturing facility	– Global leader – Key skills and expertise in the fields of manufacturing and marketing quality control

Table 7.2. Commitments of both partners of alliance IOTA

7.1.4. Perimeter of activity of the alliance

The roles and missions of each partner are specified in the contract clauses of the alliance. "We have a generic contract which details all access to tools, documentation, etc. The agreement also specifies the manufacturing techniques, prices, necessary skills, confidentiality, exchange of documents, etc.", the Tunisian project leader explains, while the Tunisian Activities director states: "The contract specifies the object of the relationship, each partner's obligations, the nature of their services, the length of the contract, the prices, the materials, the regulatory conditions, social legislation, industrial and intellectual property, confidentiality, responsibilities, hygiene and safety, shipment fees".

The contract dictates that the Tunisian partner must provide the facilities, recruit and train engineers according to abilities required by the MNC and comply with delays and recommendations set by the latter. "The contract defines our business model. We provide our partner with materials and human resources and ensure the training necessary for the advancement of the project", states the Tunisian technical director. On an operational level, the host partner has no room for maneuverability and must follow the MNC's orders to the letter. "When our partner asks us to realize a project, we must employ any technical and staff resources to execute it as requested", the Tunisian Activities director tells us. Meanwhile, the MNC must provide its ally with all details surrounding the project, supervise its progress and provide technical assistance.

Furthermore, the Tunisian company digitizes all of its management and function procedures, because of, in part, the use of an automated reporting system that monitors the progress of the project. "Our partner has direct access to the project. To improve the work of our teams and save time that would otherwise be dedicated to daily or weekly reporting, we created a tool which grants our partner access to information in real time", states the Tunisian project leader.

This is confirmed by the Tunisian software coordinator: "Our partner is pleased with the tool we created, as it results in considerable time gain and improves pertinent decision-making to advance the project".

1	Design
2	Quality control
3	Assembly

Table 7.3. *Perimeter of the alliance*

7.1.5. *Governance model of the alliance*

At an organizational level, each project leader on the Tunisian side has a counterpart at the French company. "Every Project Manager in the Tunisian company has a counterpart in France considering we have seven ongoing projects and only one line of communication", explains the Tunisian Activities director. On the Tunisian side, the Tunisian Activities director states: "We have one person with which the Project Manager interacts with on the project. This person coordinates all tasks as well as the staff involved with the project. They are the partner's counterpart, and are then referred to as the function leader". As for the French partner, it calls upon a project coordinator to monitor the progress of the schedule and the realization of any agreed-upon objectives and actions. To ensure the management of activities within the alliance, both project managers meet every 3 months. "The function leader is obligated to meet every three months with his or her interface in order to review the progress of the project", explains the Tunisian project leader.

Control is therefore exerted through frequent and regular audits. The MNC proceeded, upon signing the contract with the local company, to an audit to assess the existence of potential environmental liabilities, or any sensitive or hazardous surrounding areas. The construction of the local site integrates the sustainable development criteria surrounding the site's construction as well as the collaborators' work conditions, the conditions of the factory and compliance with IOTA N's standards in terms of risk prevention. "Our partner performs an audit on a regular basis that covers all aspects of quality, technique and management", confirms the Tunisian Activities director. With regard to work processes, the MNC makes sure the code of ethics and business practices are respected by its Tunisian partner.

Outside of formal governance mechanisms, the Tunisian company has managed to reinforce cohesion with its counterpart. "The partner proceeded to negotiate a more advantageous position in the project since they saved on time with no loss of quality. Therefore, there is greater trust, quality and placements in this relationship", the Tunisian software coordinator points out. Furthermore, the training and trips performed between Tunisia and France ensure that the mastery and use of skills play an important role within the governance of this alliance. In the early stages of this alliance, personnel training within the local company was performed by the MNC who allocated large budgets to updating and improving the Tunisian engineers' skills and competencies. "It goes both ways: an instructor comes to us to give the training session, or our engineers go to a different country to attend training on a new technology", states the Tunisian Activities director. Today, the instructors are primarily Tunisian and have received the training from the partner. "Nowadays, we are in charge of recruiting and training our engineers who will be working on the project, and are capable of providing these courses ourselves", explains the Tunisian Activities director.

Formal governance mechanisms	Standardization of qualifications (recruiting engineers) Regular audits Complying with specification sheets
Informal governance mechanisms	Visits, training performed on-site at the Tunisian company

Table 7.4. *Governance mechanisms of alliance IOTA*

7.2. Role of IS within alliance IOTA

On an informational level, IOTA N has an SAP-style ERP software package at their disposal, which results in a totally integrated system and centralizes the company's multiple functions. This solution has been adapted to all of the specific departments within IOTA N. "The majority of modules in the company are integrated in the SAP. We have also attached complementary modules for the decision-making panel and for our sales-force management. We have other solutions used to manage sales previsions, inventory management, etc.", the French Project coordinator confirms.

This same partner has also created a digital joint work solution to allow the joint monitoring of the project's progress and share information instantly with its partner which states, under the leadership of its Activities director, while also mentioning its partner's IS: "We can access the project from our partner's IS via Google. The partner suggested this solution in order to monitor all things pertaining to emails, dashboards, reporting, information tools etc. Our integration into this IS is only recent. Before that, there were only email exchanges. Nowadays, all documents necessarily pass through this system". What's more, it offers the ability to capitalize one's key knowledge and best practices via a specific web portal while granting access to the Tunisian partner. "Capitalizing knowledge allows us to save 10% of time dedicated to administrative work", considers the French Project coordinator. "Our partner proceeds to the capitalization of its knowledge through a unique platform. If we encounter problems, the latter will grant us access to knowledge from former projects, past experiences, obtained results and adapted solutions, etc.", adds the Tunisian Activities director.

Furthermore, the Tunisian company is equipped with an information system that is aligned with its strategic choices. The partner's integration into its IS remains a determining element in the governance of joint projects and according to the technical director: "The need to find a converging solution of both information systems and enable better cooperation". "Our IS is configurable to the integration of joint-projects with the partner and the use of workflow tools", the Tunisian Activities director also points out. Furthermore, the local company has implemented an ERP-style software package to centralize its functions. "Our company uses various systems for accounts-payable, accounting, invoicing, human resource management, project management, procedure management, skills management, etc., most of which are integrated into our ERP", the Tunisian technical director confirms.

On a cross-organization level, the tools used for communicating and sharing information play a key role in decision making and the quality of collaboration between partners. "Collaboration requires collaborative and information-sharing tools that are included in our IS, such as video-conferences. These tools are essential to the durability of our alliance", states the Tunisian technical director. Thus, integrating these tools allows the partners to alleviate problems arising from coordination issues and information asymmetry, which improves interaction within the project.

"Our partner always needs to have access to information in real-time. On our end, we need to guarantee its reliability, relevance and efficiency", states the Tunisian technical director who goes on to say: "We make sure we maintain interactivity by all means of communication such as email, telephone, extranet, SharePoint, etc.".

The implementation of an EDI by the partners adds perceived value, as IOTA S' Software coordinator explains: "Implementing an EDI has been very well received by our partner, as it simplifies a lot of tasks. Personnel using this technology will save time dedicated to proofing and validating, and will, thus, use that time for other tasks. User analysis will be more in-depth since it includes a tie-gain and subsequently, a more careful and broader analysis".

During the early stages of the alliance, the Tunisian partner made its reports on an Excel spreadsheet, inputting information manually. Reporting was a long and tedious task. It was also very prone to errors during these inputs, which resulted in gaps between the digital representation of these data and the real progression of the project. "In the beginning of our relationship, we would make typical Excel reports. As time went on, we began to realize that this was a long and tedious process that wouldn't work with our partner's expectations", states the Tunisian Activities director, before adding: "The partner was concerned about the amount of time it was taking to gather information they needed for the continuation of activities. What's more, this time-loss resulted in sequential losses of information and its relevance".

Therefore, the partner benefitted from having an overview of all project phases in terms of progression, scheduling, eventual recruitment of engineers, technical sheets, weekly meetings, etc. Also, the reports are based around a number of indicators that are specified by the French specification sheet. "The reporting is based around a number of indicators surrounding productivity, deadlines, problems encountered, etc. All of these indicators are stated in the specification sheet", states the Tunisian technical director, whose statement is followed up by the software coordinator who says: "The partner's internal specification sheet includes all project specifications-confidential information communicated in a coded format to preserve their knowledge". Reporting enables the analysis of technical indicators and monitoring of action plans by the French partner. "The French partner is made aware of any modifications that impact the project and its progress. The latter can collect metrics that it considers useful for internal reporting on any delays, time management, performed or non-accomplished tasks, resource and responsibility distribution", explains the Tunisian Activities director.

The IS plays an important role in coordinating tasks for the project team, assigning each individual to his or her role and the instructions they should follow. It also filters information, meaning it makes sure that the right information reaches the appropriate users, thus avoiding errors or disturbances. "Tasks are managed through the IS by creating and assigning them to the operators involved in the project. They do not always have access to the same overview of the work. If one person is not involved in the project, he or she will not be able to view the project. Distributing a piece of information must always respect the characteristics of reliability, relevance, and usefulness. If the IS broadcasts useless information, this can disturb users and create time-loss. It is important that information remains useful and useable", explain the Tunisian Technical director.

On an informed level, the IS enables remote training courses, thanks to e-learning, which plays a crucial role in providing knowledge for the benefit of the host partner. "Many training sessions are performed remotely. Our group has a videoconference system, a space dedicated to screen-sharing, information knowledge. It's a virtual meeting with the partner who approves the sharing of a large amount of knowledge", explains the Tunisian project leader. Therefore, the IS allows the transfer, sharing and capitalization of knowledge for the host partner. "The IS enables the capitalization of knowledge. When we encounter problems, the partner grants us access to the Google portal on which are indexed the best practices and past experiences. We can easily find solutions to encountered difficulties and reason via analogy by adopting proposed solutions on the site", states the Activities director, to which the project manager adds: "The partner shares slideshows of its trainings and presentations on the Google portal by giving us access on demand".

	Case ALPHA	Case DELTA	Case KAPPA	Case IOTA
Ends sought by each party	The European partner: Geographic expansion The Tunisian partner: Acquiring new skills in the fields of manufacturing, R&D, marketing Expanding their range of products	The European partner: Reducing manufacturing costs Adapting to local regulations The Tunisian partner: Acquiring a new skill in the field of manufacturing	The European partner: Reducing transaction costs Geographic expansion Adapting to local regulations The Tunisian partner: Acquiring new skills in the fields of manufacturing and marketing	The European partner : Reducing transaction costs Use local workforce The Tunisian partner : Acquiring new skills

Resources committed by the partners	The European partner: Transfer of skills relating to supply (improving the quality of raw materials) Transfer of marketing skills (new ad campaigns, expansion of the partner's product range, new commercial communications actions) Transfer of technical skills (new manufacturing processes and techniques) Transfer of R&D skills (designing new recipes suitable with the evolution of Tunisian consumers' tastes and expectations) Solid financial basis The Tunisian partner: Brand image Contextual knowledge Access to manufacturing sites and equipment Access to qualified personnel A large and competitive distribution network	The European partner: High-end brand image Transfer of technical skills The Tunisian partner: Access to a manufacturing site and quality control lab Access to qualified personnel	The European partner: High-end brand image Transfer of technical skills The Tunisian partner: Access to a manufacturing site and quality control lab Access to qualified personnel Access to a large and competitive distribution network	The European partner : High-end brand image Transfer of technical skills The Tunisian partner : Access to an equipped manufacturing site Access to competent labor
Perimeter of activity of the alliance	Creation of a new organizational unit characterized by the integration of different specialties of the alliance (manufacturing, commercialization, finance, marketing and R&D)	Creation of a new organizational unit characterized by the integration of manufacturing activities, quality control of the MNC's drugs	Integration of manufacturing and distribution activities of licensed products onto the Tunisian market	Integration of manufacturing, quality control and automotive component assembly activities

Management of the alliance and role of IS	Audits/Implementation of a governance committee /Presence of foreign personnel at the positions of Marketing Director and Deputy CEO Implementation of a reporting system on a number of financial indicators specified by the MNC and are transferred to them regularly Regular and frequent communications during daily interactions, personal and management visits thanks to typical communication tools (e-mails, telephone) IOIS (web conferences, videoconferences, joint platforms) Development of a new ERP system resulting of the alliance integrating all alliance activities accessible to all actors involved in the JV	Standardizati on of norms in terms of manufactur-ing, quality control of products/ audits visits and meetings and meetings between partners; on-site training Implementati on of a reporting system on a number of financial indicators specified by the MNC that are transferred to them regularly	Complying with manufacturing and distribution processes for the licensed product/ complying with contractual clauses Informal communication between partners during visits and videoconferences Implementation of a reporting system on a number of financial indicators specified by the MNC that are transferred to them regularly	Implementation of a reporting system on a number of financial indicators specified by the MNC that are transferred to them regularly Complying with the European partner's instructions during recruitment and workforce training/ complying with manufacturing and quality control process for automotive components required by the MNC/informal communication between partners during visits; videoconferenc es; on-site training/use of an EDI authorizing greater activity

Table 7.5. *Synthesis table*

Conclusion

The Role of IS in Managing Asymmetric Alliances

The rise in uncertainty generated by the acceleration of economic rhythms combined with political tensions and strong competitive tendencies in the Mediterranean area are not without consequences for Southern companies that are increasingly looking to progress in an evolving economic space. Bewildered by an increasingly ambiguous and uncertain environment, the latter have rushed to bind themselves into strategic alliances with their Northern counterparts to reinforce their current and future competitive presence. The durability of these asymmetric alliances is largely tribute to their partners' abilities to implement governance tools in their partnership, which is where information systems become key components.

In this vein, we have seen through a number of case studies how the partners of these alliances have been able to mobilize their information systems to overcome difficulties relating to technological asymmetry, geography and cultures. The reference frames in use, both theoretical and managerial, to analyze the different cases of alliances, have allowed us to contrast the specificities of the role played by IS in the management of these asymmetric alliances.

In the following sections, we expose the conclusions that can be drawn from these case studies with regard to the contributions of IS in managing these alliances.

A motor for improving communications within and across businesses

Communication is one of the most important activities within strategic alliances [CHE 01]. The four case studies in the previous chapters show how the use of information systems substantially improves communications between strategic partners. The use of information processing systems allows companies to solve issues relating to ambiguity and uncertainty and easily establish a common interpretation between partners. Uncertainty is considered to be the result of a lack of information. This can be reduced by emphasizing exchanges of information by using traditional tools such as written reports, but also audiovisual media that combine voice and image transmissions. Information systems therefore allow users to exchange points of view, sentiments and interpretations thanks to a combination of audiovisual media selected for their ability to transmit quick and immediate feedback of multiple elements such as the tone of voice, varied language, etc.

Information technologies (for example the telephone, e-mail, video conferences, chat-rooms, EDI, or even decision-support software) emphasize communication between companies separated geographically because of their acute ability to share information in real time. The introduction of these technologies generates new links between actors, groups, activities, departments and units that become interconnected along the value chain of the alliance. The analysis of these cases (ALPHA, DELTA, KAPPA and IOTA) highlights the fact that adopting cross-organizational information systems, in particular videoconferences, considerably reduces information asymmetry and reinforces links between partners. These technologies emphasize communication in both formal and informal aspects. Aside from this, they enable the partners to exchange information, align their points of view, and therefore help achieve mutual understanding.

Thus, the use of information technologies within the strategic alliances presented in this book favor the development of a reliable organizational network based on shared information sources and interactions among different parties.

Our case studies also allow us to shed light on the managers of asymmetric alliances in terms of choice of IS adapted for coordinating joint activities, as well as efficient communication. Allied companies must, therefore, integrate digital platforms and databases before even creating their alliance in order to enhance communication and better anticipate difficulties relating to geographical distance [KAS 99].

A tool for assistance governance and relevant decision making

The analysis of the presented case studies demonstrates how the management of asymmetric strategic alliances is characterized by great complexity. The partners involved in an asymmetric alliance face elevated transaction costs due to the risk of opportunism, uncertainty and the unpredictable nature of the environment. The partners generally end up unable to assess and anticipate the contributions, objectives and behaviors of their partner, particularly when there is a wide geographical divide. Furthermore, problems linked with informational asymmetry are likely to impede the control and evaluation process of the alliance's performance.

The information system is most often used as an efficient control instrument within the alliances studied. The complexity and risks to which the asymmetric alliance is confronted lead the partner to acquire an interactive control system that relies on the use of formal information systems that allow the company to be regularly and personally involved in its partner's activities [AND 06]. The formalization thus includes standardizing plans, documents relating to decisions, actions, past experiences and models for presenting information in order to increase transparency and improve control over activities within the alliance.

First of all, implementing an ERP can guarantee the digitization and standardization of management and operation procedures within the alliance. Because of this technology, the leaders benefit from a common language surrounding the processes included in the alliance. This allows them to react rapidly to hazards that arise from supply or local markets and adapt their resources to the level of activities.

Next, the use of decisional systems (reporting, dashboards, etc.) enable better monitoring of behaviors and operations, performed by either partner and contain the negative consecutive effects of a greater asymmetry among them. A regular reporting system using a unified repository improves the governance of joint activities. This involves presenting all data using a unique standard in order to avoid incomprehension or incompatibility due to cultural and/or managerial differences. Using these tools enables them to improve transparency and traceability of managerial processes within the alliance and therefore reduces the opportunistic and non-cooperative behaviors that arise, while also ensuring better relations within the partnership.

Furthermore, the use of an EDI type IOIS by the partners allows them to coordinate the activities within the alliance [SWA 91, BER 96]. The choice of this information system is crucial due to the abundance of exchange flows between partners. The implementation of these applications allows for better interoperability between the two partners' IS and ensures greater fluidity in their exchanges.

Finally, implementing new tools such as a joint web portal allows greater traceability and product quality as well as faster feedback of information relating to sales volume to the MNC. Therefore, the partners develop the ability to exchange information more efficiently and with a greater level of interaction while granting them autonomy and independence in their operations.

The IS ability to efficiently combine and articulate these different types of technological tools therefore appears as a key factor for success in governing the asymmetric alliance. It would be difficult to monitor an alliance's progress without a sophisticated information system that supports interaction between allies. The latter assists alliance members in establishing their strategic planning, decision making and performance system. The use of information systems as a control tool for the alliance reduces, in the same way, transaction costs relating to monitoring and controlling joint activities and manipulation errors, which then reduces informational asymmetry and improves joint decision making. By acquiring an efficient interactive control system combined with a good information system, partners within an alliance are likely to see their activities coordinated better as a result of improved fluidity in their exchanges of information, also reducing the level of asymmetry between them.

A tool for managing joint knowledge

As we have seen, the use of information systems enables partners within an alliance to manage their knowledge more efficiently as it makes it easier to digitize, transfer and internalize their accumulated knowledge. The key operators are meant to regularly report to the alliance. To this effect, they are meant to keep records (in the form of a memo, note, report, or presentation) that track decisions, actions or even incidents in the alliance. Codification, therefore, refers to resources such as control lists or procedure manuals that may serve to support the management of strategic alliances. Partners can also share and transfer experiences in more informal ways through work meetings such as brainstorming sessions or group seminars that encourage informal information and experience sharing that then must be internalized by actors involved in the alliance.

By encouraging both codification and internalization of knowledge, information technologies enhance the value of data from various sources and the integration of different organizational forms, thus reinforcing the possibilities for interaction and retroaction between different actors within the alliance. Furthermore, tools for codifying knowledge improve the way it is shared and help record best practices within the alliance. This also applies to transfer tools, which allow partners to mutualize their experiences and best practices by demonstrating the procedures and tools they have developed.

The in-depth analysis of our case studies thus demonstrates that the presence of information systems within these alliances not only rationalizes decision-making processes, but also reinforces reactivity and interactions among partners. These alliances involve individual and/or collective interactions between partnering companies. Integration mechanisms for processes and applications are necessary to encourage exchanges and improve the direction of the joint venture. It becomes apparent that governance and control mechanisms for these alliances are increasingly combined with information systems that allow the flows of information to feedback and be subject to analysis in real time; and this allows partners to take faster and more appropriate decisions and actions.

This application must also be coupled with reinforced cooperation and trust among partners. Socialization and initiation processes presented in the case studies contribute to aligning perspectives between partners and thus creating favorable conditions to harmonize decision-making processes within the alliance. And yet, the information system cannot be the sole central management tool for an entire asymmetric alliance. It is increasingly called-upon to connect to a management system, as well as alliance governance and control models, to encourage the coherence of strategic choices from partners and the operational modalities of joint action.

Relying on cross-examinations of both partners of asymmetric alliances, the results of these case studies can lead to numerous managerial recommendations both during the formation of the alliance and its management.

During the formation of an asymmetric alliance, the partners must define the level of integration of an IS in coherence with their level of interdependence and the perimeter of activity of the alliance, which will be determined by the level of involvement in the alliance. It is also important for partners to define the level of integration of their IS in relation to the specificities of the value chain.

During the management phase of an asymmetric alliance, it becomes important to choose the IS that are likely to reinforce the coordination of joint activities and encourage positive communication among partners. In this vein, cross-organizational information systems play a key role in accelerating the transmission and processing of information, improving the quality of the exchanged information and, therefore, reinforcing relations between partners, something that can support an innovative dynamic in the relationship.

Faced with the necessity to efficiently articulate factors such as rationality, contingency and conscious decisions in the management of asymmetric alliances, partners increasingly resort to the use of IOIS, which are likely to ensure coherence between the different levels within and among companies. This allows key actors to collaborate and learn from one another by using information systems to create links and interactions between local and global decisions, as well as short-term and long-term decisions. The alliance will therefore be in a position to develop a form of collective intelligence allowing it to detect and process indicative signals, which could potentially influence its durability.

Bibliography

[ALT 99] ALTER S., *Information Systems: A Management Perspective*, Addison-Wesley, Boston, 1999.

[AMA 06] AMABILE S., GADILLE M., "Coopération interentreprises, système d'information et attention organisationnelle", *Revue Française de Gestion*, vol. 164, pp. 97–118, 2006.

[AND 92] ANDREU A., RICART J.E., VALOR J., *Information Systems: Strategic Planning: A Source of Competitive Advantage*, Blackwell Publishers, Florida, 1992.

[AND 06] ANDERSON S., CHRIST M., SEDATOLE K., *Managing Strategic Alliance Risk: Survey Evidence of Control Practices in Collaborative Inter-organizational Settings*, IIA Research Foundation, London, 2006.

[ASS 10] ASSENS C., CHERBIB J., "L'alliance asymétrique: une stratégie durable?", *La Revue des Sciences de Gestion*, vol. 243–244, pp. 111–121, 2010.

[BAR 91] BARNEY J., "Firm resources and sustained competitive advantage", *Journal of Management*, vol. 17, no. 1, pp. 99–120, 1991.

[BAR 82] BARRETT S., KONSYNSKI B., "Inter-organization information sharing systems", *Management Information Systems Quarterly*, vol. 6, pp. 93–105, 1982.

[BEA 05] BEAMISH P.W., JUNG J.C., "The performance and Survival of joint-ventures with parents of asymmetric size", *Management International*, vol. 10, no. 1, pp. 19–30, 2005.

[BEL 01] BELLON B., BENYOUSSEF A., PLUNKET A., "Les déterminants des alliances industrielles stratégiques Nord-Sud: quelques enseignements tirées des alliances euroméditerranéennes", *IIe conférence du Femise*, Marseille, 2001.

[BHA 13] BHARADWAJ A., EL SAWI O., PAVLOU P.A. *et al.*, "Digital business strategy: toward a next generation of insights", *Management Information Systems Quarterly*, vol. 37, no. 2, pp. 471–482, 2013.

[BLA 06] BLANCHOT F., "Alliances et performances: un essai de synthèse", *Cahiers de recherche CREPA/DRM*, vol. 1, Université Paris Dauphine, January 2006.

[BRI 13] BRION S., MOTHE C., PERERA C., "La contribution des TIC et du présentiel à l'efficacité de la coordination des équipes projets de NPD distribuées", *Système d'Information et management*, vol. 18, no. 4, pp. 43–75, 2013.

[BUC 88] BUCKLEY P.J., CASSON M., "A theory of cooperation in international business", in CONTRACTOR F.J., LORANGE P. (eds), *Cooperative Strategies in International Business*, Lexington Books, Lanham, 1988.

[BUC 93] BUCKLIN L.P., SENGUPTA S., "Organizing successful co-marketing alliances", *Journal of Marketing*, vol. 57, pp. 32–46, 1993.

[CHA 02] CHARLOT J.-M., LANCINI A., "De la connaissance aux systèmes, Information supports", in ROWE F. (ed.), *Faire de la recherche en systèmes d'information*, Vuibert, Paris, 2002.

[CHE 02] CHEN H., CHEN T.-T.-J., "Asymmetric strategic alliances A network view", *Journal of Business Research*, vol. 55, pp. 1007–1013, 2002.

[CHE 03] CHEN H., CHEN T.-T.-J., "Governance structures in strategic alliances: transaction cost versus resource-based perspective", *Journal of World Business,* vol. 38, pp. 1–14, 2003.

[CHE 01] CHENG W.L., LI H., LOVE E.D. *et al.*, "Network communication in the construction industry", *Corporate Communications: An International Journal*, vol. 6, no. 2, pp. 61–70, 2001.

[CHE 14a] CHERBIB J., CHERIET F., "L'instabilité des alliances stratégiques asymétriques : une option programmée par la firme multinationale", *Revue internationale PME*, vol. 27, no. 2, pp. 15–38, 2014.

[CHE 08] CHERIET F., LEROY F., RASTOIN J.L., "Instabilité des alliances stratégiques asymétriques: cas des entreprises agroalimentaires en Méditerranée", *Management International*, vol. 12, no. 3, pp. 45–46, 2008.

[CHE 14b] CHERIET F., DIKMEN L., "Contrat ou confiance: effet de la gouvernance sur les performances des alliances stratégiques asymétriques", *La Revue des Sciences de Gestion*, no. 266, pp. 43–51, 2014.

[CHR 05] CHRYSOSTOME E., BEAMISH P., HEBERT L. *et al.*, "Les alliances asymétriques: Réflexions sur une forme complexe de coopération", *Management International*, vol. 10, no. 1, pp. 1–17, 2005.

[COA 37] COASE R.H., "The nature of the firm", *Economica*, vol. 4, no. 16, pp. 386–405, 1937.

[COH 90] COHEN W.M., LEVINTHAL D.A., "Absorptive capacity: a new perspective on learning and innovation", *Administrative Science Quarterly*, vol. 35, no. 1, pp. 128–152, 1990.

[COL 03] COLOMBO M.G., "Alliance form: a test of the contractual and competence perspectives", *Strategic Management Journal*, vol. 24, pp. 1209–1229, 2003.

[CON 88] CONTRACTOR F.J., LORANGE P., "Why should firms cooperate? The strategy and economics basis for cooperative ventures", in CONTRACTOR F.J., LORANGE P. (eds), *Cooperative Strategies in International Business*, Lexington Books, Lanham, 1988.

[COU 99] COURBON J.-C., TAJAN S., *Groupware et intranet. Vers le partage des connaissances*, Dunod, Paris, 1999.

[CRI 03] CRIE D., "De l'extraction des connaissances au knowledge management", *Revue française de gestion*, vol. 5, no. 146, pp. 59–79, 2003.

[DAS 98] DAS T.K., TENG B.S., "Between trust and control: developing confidence in partner cooperation in alliances", *Academy Management Review*, vol. 123, pp. 491–513, 1998.

[DAS 99] DAS T.K., TENG B.S., "Managing risks in strategic alliances", *Academy of Management Executive*, vol. 13, no. 4, pp. 50–62, 1999.

[DAS 00] DAS T.K., TENG B.S., "Instabilities of strategic alliances: an internal tensions perspective", *Organization Science*, vol. 11, no. 1, pp. 77–101, 2000.

[DAS 08] DAS T.K., TENG B.S., "Governance structure choice in strategic alliances: the roles of alliance objectives, alliance management experience, and international partners", *Management Decision*, vol. 46, no. 5, pp. 725–742, 2008.

[DEL 08] DELMOND M.-H., PETIT Y., GAUTIER J.-M., *Management des Systèmes d'Information*, Dunod, Paris, 2008.

[DIK 10] DIKMEN L., Les déterminants de la performance des joint-ventures internationales entre pays développés et pays émergeants: le cas de la Turquie, PhD Thesis, University of Montpellier, 2010.

[DON 05] DONADA C., NOGATCHEWSKY G., "Dépendance asymétrique dans les alliances verticales: comment un client vassal contrôle-t-il ses fournisseurs?", *Management International*, vol. 10, no. 1, pp. 63–74, 2005.

[DOZ 88] DOZ Y.L., *Technology Partnerships between Larger and Smaller Firms: Some Critical Issues,* in CONTRACTOR F.J., LORANGE P. (eds), *Cooperative Strategies in International Business*, Lexington Books, Lanham, 1988.

[DOZ 89] DOZ Y.L., HAMEL G., PRAHALAD C.K., "Collaborate with your competitor and win", *Harvard Business Review*, vol. 67, pp. 133–139, 1989.

[DOZ 98] DOZ Y.L., HAMEL G., *Alliance Advantages*, Harvard Business School Press, Boston, 1998.

[DRO 06] DROGENDIJK R., SLANGEN A., "Hofstede, Schwartz, or managerial perceptions: the effects of various cultural distance measures on establishment mode choices by multinational enterprises", *International Business Review*, vol. 15, no. 4, pp. 361–380, 2006.

[GAL 73] GALBRAITH J., *Designing Complex Organizations*, Addison-Wesley, Boston, 1973.

[GAR 95] GARRETTE B., DUSSAUGE P., *Les stratégies d'alliance*, Editions d'Organisation, Paris, 1995.

[GUI 04] GUILLOUZO R., THEPAUT Y., "Une interprétation de la coopération interentreprises en termes de pouvoir informationnel", *La revue des sciences de gestion*, vol. 206, pp. 41–60, 2004.

[GUL 95] GULATI R., "Does familiarity breed trust? The implications of repeated ties for contractual choice in alliances", *Academy of Management Journal*, vol. 38, pp. 85–112, 1995.

[GUL 98] GULATI R., SINGH H., "The architecture of cooperation: managing coordination costs and appropriation concerns in strategic alliances", *Administrative Science Quarterly*, vol. 43, pp. 781–814, 1998.

[HAG 96] HAGEDOORN J., NARULA R., "Choosing organizational modes of strategic technology partnering: international and sectoral differences", *Journal of International Business Studies*, vol. 27, pp. 265–284, 1996.

[HAG 02] HAGEDOORN J., "Inter-firm R&D partnerships: an overview of major trends and patterns since 1960", *Research Policy*, vol. 31, pp. 477–492, 2002.

[HAR 85] HARRIGAN K.R., *Strategies for Joint-Ventures*, Lexington Books, Lanham, 1985.

[HEN 88] HENNART J.-F., "A transaction cost theory of equity joint-ventures", *Strategic Management Journal*, vol. 9, no. 4, pp. 361–374, 1988.

[HOL 05] HOLTBRÜGGE D., "Configuration and coordination of value activities in German Multinational Corporations", *European Management Journal*, vol. 23, pp. 564–575, 2005.

[HYD 99] HYDER A.S., "Differences between developed and developing country joint-ventures: a reality or myth?", *International Business Review*, vol. 8, pp. 441–461, 1999.

[INK 97] INKPEN A.C., BEAMISH P.W., "Knowledge, bargaining power and the instability of international joint-venture", *Academy Management Review*, vol. 22, pp. 177–202, 1997.

[INK 04] INKPEN A.C., CURRALL S.C., "The coevolution of trust, control, and learning in joint-ventures", *Organization Science*, vol. 15, pp. 586–599, 2004.

[JEA 14] JEAN-AMANS C., ABDELLATIF M., "Modes d'implantation des PME à l'étranger: le choix entre filiale 100% et coentreprise internationale", *Management International*, vol. 18, no. 2, pp. 195–208, 2014.

[JEN 76] JENSEN M.C., MECKLING W.H., "Theory of the firm: managerial behavior, agency costs and ownership structure", *Journal of Financial Economics*, vol. 3, no. 4, pp. 305–360, 1976.

[JOL 01] JOLLY D., "France-Chine – joint-ventures et transferts technologiques", *Revue Française de Gestion*, vol. 133, pp. 32–48, 2001.

[KAS 99] KASIK D.J., KIMBALL C.E., FELT J.L. *et al.*, "A flexible approach to alliances of complex applications", *Proceedings of the 21st International Conference on Software Engineering*, Los Angeles, pp. 23–32, 1999.

[KEF 10] KEFI H., "Mesures perceptuelles de l'usage des systèmes d'information: application de la théorie du comportement planifié", *Humanisme et Entreprise*, vol. 297, pp. 41–65, 2010.

[KHA 98] KHANNA T., GULATI R., NOHRIA N., "The dynamics of learning alliances: competition, cooperation, and relative scope", *Strategic Management Journal*, vol. 19, pp. 193–210, 1998.

[KOC 10] KOCOGLU Y., MOATTY F., "Diffusion et combinaison des TIC au sein des entreprises en 2006: les réseaux, la gestion des données et l'intégration par les ERP", *Réseaux*, vol. 162, pp. 37–72, 2010.

[KOG 88a] KOGUT B., "Joint-ventures: theoretical and empirical perspectives", *Strategic Management Journal*, vol. 9, pp. 319–332, 1988.

[KOG 88b] KOGUT B., SINGH H., "The effect of national culture on the choice of entry mode", *Journal of International Business Studies*, vol. 19, no. 3, pp. 411–432, 1988.

[KUM 96] KUMAR K., VAN DISSEL H.G., "Sustainable collaboration: managing conflict and cooperation in interorganizational systems", *MIS Quarterly*, vol. 20, no. 3, pp. 279–300, 1996.

[LAU 15] LAUDON K.C., LAUDON J.P., *Management Information Systems: Managing the Digital Firm*, Prentice Hall, Upper Saddle River, 2015.

[LEC 13] LECLERCQ-VANDELANNOITTE A., ISAAC H., "Technologies de l'information, contrôle et panoptique: pour une approche deleuzienne", *Système d'information et Management*, vol. 18, no. 2, pp. 9–36, 2013.

[LEC 84] LECRAW D.J., "Bargaining power, ownership and profitability of transnational corporations in developing countries", *Journal of International Business Studies*, vol. 26, no. 3, pp. 637–654, 1984.

[LEE 03] LEE J.R., CHEN W.R., KAO C., "Determinants and performance impact of asymmetric governance structure in international joint-venture: an empirical investigation", *Journal of Business Research*, vol. 56, pp. 815–828, 2003.

[LU 06] LU J., BEAMISH P.W., "Partnering strategies and performance of SMEs' international joint-ventures", *Journal of Business Venturing*, vol. 21, no. 4, pp. 461–486, 2006.

[MAK 98] MAKINO S., BEAMISH P.W., "Performance and survival with joint-ventures with non-conventional ownership structures", *Journal of International Business Studies*, vol. 29, no. 4, pp. 797–818, 1998.

[MAR 89] MARTINEZ J.I., JARILLO J.C., "The evolution of research on coordination mechanisms in multinational corporations", *Journal of International Business Studies*, vol. 20, no. 3, pp. 489–514, 1989.

[MEI 10] MEIER O., MISSONIER A., "Alliance asymétrique: comment conclure un accord gagnant-gagnant? Les sources de persuasion des dirigeants", in GUNDOLF K., MEIER O., MISSONIER A. (eds), *Négociation et stratégies d'entreprises*, Hermès-Lavoisier, Paris, 2010.

[MEN 97] MENARD C., "Le Pilotage des formes organisationnelles hybrides," *Revue Economique*, vol. 48, no. 3, pp. 741–750, 1997.

[MIL 96] MILLER R.R., GLEN J.D., JASPERSEN F.Z. *et al.*, "International joint-ventures in developing countries: Happy marriages?", *International Finance Corporation*, vol. 26, The World Bank, Washington D.C., 1996.

[MIN 82] MINTZBERG H., *Structure et dynamique des organisations*, Editions d'Organisation, Paris, 1982.

[MIT 00] MITCHELL W., GARRETTE B., DUSSAUGE P., "Learning from competing partners: outcomes and durations of scale and link alliances in Europe, North America and Asia", *Strategic Management Journal*, vol. 21, no. 2, pp. 99–126, 2000.

[MJO 97] MJOEN H., TALLMAN S., "Control and performance in international joint-ventures", *Organization Science*, vol. 8, no. 3, pp. 257–274, 1997.

[MOU 05] MOULINE A., "Symétrie et asymétrie des alliances dans une industrie en mutation: le cas des télécommunications", *Revue Management International*, vol. 10, pp. 76–87, 2005.

[MOW 96] MOWERY D.C., OXLEY J.E., SILVERMAN B.S., "Strategic alliances and interfirm knowledge transfer", *Strategic Management Journal*, vol. 17, pp. 77–91, 1996.

[O'DW 05] O'DWYER M., O'FLYNN E., "MNC-SME strategic alliances: a model framing knowledge value as the primary predictor of governance modal choice", *Journal of International Management*, vol. 11, no. 3, pp. 397–416, 2005.

[OXL 97] OXLEY J.E., "Appropriability hazards and governance in strategic alliances: a transaction cost approach", *Journal of Law, Economics and Organization*, vol. 13, pp. 387–409, 1997.

[PAR 96] PARK S.H., RUSSO M.V., "When competition eclipses cooperation: an event history analysis of joint-venture failure", *Management Science*, vol. 42, no. 6, pp. 875–890, 1996.

[PAR 93] PARKHE A., "Partner nationality and the structure-performance relationship in strategic alliances", *Organization Science*, vol. 4, pp. 301–324, 1993.

[PFE 78] PFEFFER J., SALANCIK G., *The External Control of Organizations: A Resource dependence Perspective*, Harper & Row, New York, 1978.

[PIS 89] PISANO G.P., "Using equity participation to support exchange: evidence from the biotechnology industry", *Journal of Law, Economics and Organization*, vol. 5, no. 1, pp. 109–126, 1989.

[POR 86] PORTER M.E., FULLER M.B., "Coalitions and global strategy", *Competition in Global Industries*, Harvard Business School Press, Boston, 1986.

[PRA 90] PRAHALAD C.K., HAMEL G., "The core competence of the corporation", *Harvard Business Review*, vol. 68, no. 3, pp. 79–91, 1990.

[PUT 96] PUTHOD D., "Alliances et PME: un diagnostic", *Revue Française de Gestion*, no. 110, pp. 30–45, 1996.

[RAY 96] RAYMOND L., BERGERON F., "EDI dans la PME et la grande entreprise: similitudes et différences", *Revue Internationale PME*, vol. 9, no. 1, pp. 41–60, 1996.

[REI 02] REIX R., "Changements organisationnels et technologies de l'information", *Cahiers du CREGO*, vol. 12, University Montpellier II, 2002.

[REI 11] REIX R., FALLERY B., KALIKA M. *et al.*, *Systèmes d'information et management des organisations*, Vuibert, Paris, 2011.

[SAÏ 06] SAÏD K., "Le transfert de compétences au sein des alliances interentreprises euroméditerranéennes en question", *Revue des Sciences de Gestion*, vol. 4, pp. 220–221, 2006.

[SIM 04] SIMONIN B.L., "An empirical investigation of the process of knowledge transfer in international strategic alliances", *Journal of International Business Studies*, vol. 35, pp. 407–427, 2004.

[SUO 91] SUOMI R., "Evaluation des possibilités des systèmes informatisés interorganisationnels sur la base de l'approche des coûts de transaction", *Technologie de l'Information et Société*, vol. 3, nos. 2–3, pp. 139–161, 1991.

[SUR 09] SURPLY J., "Coopération interentreprises Nord-Sud: le transfert de savoirs", *Revue Française de Gestion*, vol. 1, no. 191, pp. 49–69, 2009.

[SWA 91] SWATMAN E.M., SWATMAN P.M., "Integrating EDI into the organization's system: a model of the stages of integration", *Proceeding of the 12th International Conference on Information Systems*, New York, 1991.

[SZU 96] SZULANSKI G., "Exploring internal stickiness: impediments to the transfer of best practice within the firm", *Strategic Management Journal*, vol. 17, pp. 27–43, 1996.

[TEE 86] TEECE D., "Profiting from technological innovation: implications for integration, collaboration, licensing and public policy", *Research Policy*, vol. 15, pp. 285–305, 1986.

[TEE 97] TEECE D., PISANO G., SHUEN A., "Dynamic capabilities and strategic management", *Strategic Management Journal*, vol. 18, no. 7, pp. 509–534, 1997.

[THO 93] THOMAS J.B., TREVINO L.K., "Information processing in strategic alliance building: a multiple-case approach", *Journal of Management Studies*, vol. 30, pp. 779–814, 1993.

[TIN 05] TINLOT G., MOTHE C., "Alliance asymétrique et pouvoir de négociation des partenaires", *Revue Management International*, vol. 10, pp. 31–49, 2005.

[VER 09] VERNADAT F.B., "Enterprise integration and interoperability", in NOF S.Y. (ed.), *Springer Handbook of Automation*, pp. 1529–1538, Springer, Berlin, 2009.

[VID 05] VIDOT-DELERUE H., SIMON E., "Confiance, contrat et degré d'asymétrie dans les contrats d'alliances", *Management International*, vol. 10, no. 1, pp. 51–62, 2005.

[WIL 85] WILLIAMSON O.E., *The Economic Institutions of Capitalism: Firms, Markets, Relational Contracting*, Free Press, New York, 1985.

[WIL 91] WILLIAMSON O.E., "Strategizing, economizing and economic organization", *Strategic Management Journal*, vol. 12, pp. 75–94, 1991.

[YAN 94] YAN A., GRAY B., "Bargaining power, management control, and performance in United States-China joint-venture: a comparative case study", *Academy of Management Journal*, vol. 37, pp. 1478–1517, 1994.

[YIN 09] YIN R.K., *Case Study Research, Design and Methods*, Sage Publishing, London, 2009.

[ZAH 95] ZAHEER A., VENKATRAMAN N., "Relational governance as an interorganizational strategy: an empirical test of the role of trust in economic exchange", *Strategic Management Journal*, vol. 16, no. 5, pp. 373–392, 1995.

Index

Other titles from

in

Information Systems, Web and Pervasive Computing

2017

LESAS Anne-Marie, MIRANDA Serge
The Art and Science of NFC Programming
(Intellectual Technologies Set – Volume 3)

SZONIECKY Samuel, BOUHAÏ Nasreddine
Collective Intelligence and Digital Archives: Towards Knowledge
Ecosystems
(Digital Tools and Uses Set – Volume 1)

REYES-GARCIA Everardo, BOUHAÏ Nasreddine
Designing Interactive Hypermedia Systems
(Digital Tools and Uses Set – Volume 2)

2016

BEN CHOUIKHA Mona
Organizational Design for Knowledge Management

BERTOLO David
Interactions on Digital Tablets in the Context of 3D Geometry Learning
(Human-Machine Interaction Set – Volume 2)

BOUVARD Patricia, SUZANNE Hervé
Collective Intelligence Development in Business

DAUPHINÉ André
Geographical Models in Mathematica

EL FALLAH SEGHROUCHNI Amal, ISHIKAWA Fuyuki, HÉRAULT Laurent, TOKUDA Hideyuki
Enablers for Smart Cities

FABRE Renaud, in collaboration with MESSERSCHMIDT-MARIET Quentin, HOLVOET Margot
New Challenges for Knowledge

GAUDIELLO Ilaria, ZIBETTI Elisabetta
Learning Robotics, with Robotics, by Robotics
(Human-Machine Interaction Set – Volume 3)

HENROTIN Joseph
The Art of War in the Network Age
(Intellectual Technologies Set – Volume 1)

KITAJIMA Munéo
Memory and Action Selection in Human–Machine Interaction
(Human–Machine Interaction Set – Volume 1)

LAGRAÑA Fernando
E-mail and Behavioral Changes: Uses and Misuses of Electronic Communications

LEIGNEL Jean-Louis, UNGARO Thierry, STAAR Adrien
Digital Transformation

NOYER Jean-Max
Transformation of Collective Intelligences
(Intellectual Technologies Set – Volume 2)

VENTRE Daniel
Information Warfare – 2nd edition

VITALIS André
The Uncertain Digital Revolution

2015

ARDUIN Pierre-Emmanuel, GRUNDSTEIN Michel, ROSENTHAL-SABROUX Camille
Information and Knowledge System
(Advances in Information Systems Set – Volume 2)

BÉRANGER Jérôme
Medical Information Systems Ethics

BRONNER Gérald
Belief and Misbelief Asymmetry on the Internet

IAFRATE Fernando
From Big Data to Smart Data
(Advances in Information Systems Set – Volume 1)

KRICHEN Saoussen, BEN JOUIDA Sihem
Supply Chain Management and its Applications in Computer Science

NEGRE Elsa
Information and Recommender Systems
(Advances in Information Systems Set – Volume 4)

POMEROL Jean-Charles, EPELBOIN Yves, THOURY Claire
MOOCs

SALLES Maryse
Decision-Making and the Information System
(Advances in Information Systems Set – Volume 3)

SAMARA Tarek
ERP and Information Systems: Integration or Disintegration
(Advances in Information Systems Set – Volume 5)

2014

DINET Jérôme
Information Retrieval in Digital Environments

HÉNO Raphaële, CHANDELIER Laure
3D Modeling of Buildings: Outstanding Sites

THERIAULT Marius, DES ROSIERS François
Modeling Urban Dynamics

2009

BONNET Pierre, DETAVERNIER Jean-Michel, VAUQUIER Dominique
*Sustainable IT Architecture: the Progressive Way of Overhauling
Information Systems with SOA*

PAPY Fabrice
Information Science

RIVARD François, ABOU HARB Georges, MERET Philippe
The Transverse Information System

ROCHE Stéphane, CARON Claude
Organizational Facets of GIS

2008

BRUGNOT Gérard
Spatial Management of Risks

FINKE Gerd
Operations Research and Networks

GUERMOND Yves
Modeling Process in Geography

KANEVSKI Michael
Advanced Mapping of Environmental Data

MANOUVRIER Bernard, LAURENT Ménard
Application Integration: EAI, B2B, BPM and SOA

PAPY Fabrice
Digital Libraries

Printed and bound by CPI Group (UK) Ltd, Croydon, CR0 4YY